THE PENTATEUCH

History or Story?

Howard H. Cox

University Press of America,® Inc.
Lanham · Boulder · New York · Toronto · Oxford

University Press of America,® Inc.
4501 Forbes Boulevard
Suite 200
Lanham, Maryland 20706
UPA Acquisitions Department (301) 459-3366

PO Box 317
Oxford
OX2 9RU, UK

Library of Congress Control Number: 2004115489
ISBN 0-7618-3096-0 (paperback : alk. ppr.)

To my former students at Moravian Theological Seminary

and

to the memory of James Muilenburg

Contents

Preface

This book originated out of a desire to write down my perspective on the subject that I taught seminary students for 32 years. It has long been my concern that many people who want to understand the Bible are unaware of the great fund of information about it known to scholars. In particular, they want to know whether the biblical narratives have historical validity or bear the character of legend. What is known from archaeology and literary study is enlightening in pursuing this question. It is my intention to explore the narratives from this perspective.

After embarking on this project, I enlisted six readers, asking them to provide their critical views. Two of them are specialists in the Old Testament: Dr. Bruce Dahlberg, professor emeritus at Smith College, and Dr. George Landes, professor emeritus at Union Seminary in New York. Two of them have spent careers teaching English to college students: Dr. George Diamond, professor of English at Moravian College, and Dr. James Hepburn, professor emeritus at Bates College. Two of them are—if I may use this term—educated general readers: Robert Bush, a computer program consultant, and Laraine House, a public school teacher. All of them have provided helpful comments. I must make special mention, however, of the very extensive critiques of Dr. Landes and Dr. Hepburn throughout the entire process. I have made numerous improvements from their comments. Nevertheless, any errors or shortcomings in the book are my responsibility, for which I am to be held accountable.

Two members of my family deserve words of appreciation. My wife, Shirley, over the years, has wielded a corrective pencil on my prose, suggesting at times a more felicitous rendering, and my daughter Sara copyedited the manuscript prior to its being sent to a publisher.

This is not a theological introduction to the Old Testament. Rather, it is an attempt to understand this literature in terms of its historical setting, to assess the historical value of the literary units, and to consider whether what we read is history in our sense of the word or story that is presented in historical form. My intention is that it be an antecedent to reading the Old Testament for its inherent meaning, believing that our understanding of the background of the text will enlighten the reader with a larger perspective.

Howard H. Cox
July 1, 2004

Introduction

People who revere the Bible rarely ask the question about its origin. The first chapter, indeed the first sentence, is so daunting in expressing the overwhelming power and presence of God that we are captivated by the subject of the origin of the universe rather than that of the origin of the text. And those who are engrossed in challenging the scientific theories of the Big Bang and consequent evolution seem unaware of the literary traditions that are closely related to the early chapters of Genesis, from which the idea of creation as a theological concept is largely derived.

It is the intention of this study to assist the common reader in understanding the Old Testament narrative and narrative poetry on its own terms: its historical and cultural background, its literary form, its editing and transmission, its cultic associations; all of which bear on the question: Is it history or story? We should begin with the Bible that we hold in our hands, whatever translation it is, and ask how and why it differs from other Bibles, where it came from, and what is the nature of the text that lies behind it. What we learn about the text may be significant in forming our perception about the Bible as a resource in cultivating our faith.

The Bible has been on a journey. The development and formation of the Old Testament within the community of Israel over a period of roughly a thousand years represents the first stage of the journey. The second stage of the journey is represented in the extended traditions of some Old Testament books and personages in the Intertestamental Period. Those found in Greek manuscripts of the Old Testament are known as Apocrypha. A large collection of other books from this period came to be labeled Pseudepigrapha at the time when the Hebrew Bible was first being translated into the common languages of the Western World. The Dead Sea Scrolls include yet other books from this period. A third stage may be recognized in the formation of the New Testament within the Christian community and the Mishnah with the subsequent commentary on it, the Talmud, in the Jewish community. Both communities build upon the Hebrew Bible while incorporating their own unique theological—and, for the Christian community, historical—development.

In the Middle Ages, the Christian community in the West largely ignored the Hebrew Bible and the Greek New Testament in favor of the Latin translation known as the Vulgate. The Jewish community went to great lengths to stabilize and secure the Hebrew text against any change. In both communities, commentaries were written on the biblical books.

A great flurry of scholarly interest in the Bible in the 16th century, as a part of the Protestant Reformation, produced numerous translations from Hebrew and Greek into the common languages of western Europe. Most influential were those of Luther and Tyndale. The Jewish community also formed an edition of the Hebrew text with commentaries that became standard up until the 20th century.

The development of textual criticism in the 18th, 19th, and 20th centuries, searching for the oldest and most reliable texts, coupled with the desire for a more readable format, led to a large number of new translations in the English-speaking world, especially in the second half of the 20th century. The most important new development for the present and future is the impact of the Dead Sea Scrolls in revising the text of the Old Testament, a task the extent of which may be far-reaching. It is already apparent that the traditional exemplar, the Masoretic Text, is no longer the only text which should serve as the foundation for our translations, even if it is accorded primary status.

In the 19th and 20th centuries, a strong interest developed in the lands of the Bible and their history. The discovery of the Rosetta Stone and study of the inscriptions on the Behistun Rock unlocked ancient languages, making available the literatures of ancient Egypt and Mesopotamia for the first time. Geographical surveys of Palestine were made. Scores of biblical places were identified. The science of archaeology began with Sir Flinders Petrie utilizing typology, the evolution of object types such as walls or pottery, and stratigraphy, the levels of occupation, in dating the remains of human habitation through excavation. Numerous places have been excavated, and the combination of dated material remains and extra-biblical literature are serving to build a framework of history separate from that of the Bible.

Archaeology has developed its own time periods, which are now common to the discussion of biblical history. They are:

- ▸ **Middle Bronze Age**   2000–1550 BCE
- ▸ **Late Bronze Age**   1550–1200
- ▸ **Iron Age I**   1200–900
- ▸ **Iron Age II**   900–600
- ▸ **Persian Period (Iron III)** 600–332
- ▸ **Hellenistic or Greek Period** 332–63
- ▸ **Roman Period**   63 BCE–324 CE

Some Important Dates in the History of Israel

▸ **722 BCE**   The fall of Samaria and the Northern Kingdom
                   The destruction of the Temple and of Jerusalem

▸ **597/586/
582–538**   The Babylonian Exile

▸ **538–445**   The return of many Jews to Jerusalem
                   The Second Temple building completed
                   The Maccabean Revolt

▸ **70 CE**   The destruction of the Second Temple and of
                   Jerusalem

Given the extent to which the archaeology of the Ancient Near East and its findings have developed, all discussion of the history of Israel must relate biblical references to what is known about times, places, and personages from extra-biblical references. We can no longer identify the biblical narrative on its face value as history. In some cases, archaeology has disproved the purported factuality of a narrative account. A leading example of this is what is said about the conquest of the land of Canaan in the early chapters of Joshua. Jericho was found not to be the heavily walled city described in the biblical narrative.

> *In the case of Jericho, there was no trace of a settlement of any kind in the 13th century BCE, and the earlier Late Bronze settlement, dating to the 14th century BCE, was small and poor, almost insignificant and unfortified. There was also no sign of a destruction.*[1]

The second site mentioned as conquered in the biblical narrative, Ai, had been a ruin—which is what the name means—for centuries.

Given the discrepancy in relating the archaeological findings to this narrative, and from other examples, it is now necessary to corroborate details in narrative accounts before they can be designated history.

The storm center in the discussion of Israel's history today centers on the United Monarchy. The issue is whether or not the picture given in the biblical narrative of a vast empire under David and Solomon has credibility. David is said to rule over the whole land, from Syria in the north to Edom in the south. Solomon is made famous for his magnificent buildings, his international horse trading, and his corvee. William Dever and Israel Finkelstein, perhaps the two leading field archaeologists, differ in the dating of several large building complexes that have been excavated. Dever assigns them to the 10th century BCE, the time of Solomon. Finkelstein dates them in the 9th century BCE and relates them to the kingship of Omri and Ahab in the Northern Kingdom.

History, as it relates to the biblical narratives, is difficult to establish. There are very few extra-biblical referents to personages or to "happenings." Scholars have used what evidence is available, both literary and material, to form social and political contexts that would suggest the degree to which narratives that can be interpreted as history are plausibly historical. In the past, it was common to begin with the assumption that a narrative is historical and draw support for that assumption from references, either biblical or extra-biblical, that fill in the context. It is now recognized that this does not verify the historicity of the narrative. It may be a story that has the semblance of history. We do not label an historical novel as history but, rather, as story. On the other hand, we may not be able to deny the possible historicity of a narrative, which means no judgment can be rendered on that score. In my discussion of the biblical narratives I will use what information we have to assess their possible historicity, as far as I can go.

A century ago, the very discerning German Old Testament scholar, Hermann Gunkel, examined the literary units of Genesis in terms of their representing history or legend—his word was "saga." "History treats great public occurrences, while legend deals with things that interest the common people, with personal and private matters, and is fond of presenting even political affairs and personages so that they will attract popular attention."[2] History, he says, relies on eyewitness reporting whereas legend "depends for its material partly upon tradition and partly upon imagination."[3] In his little book on Elijah, Gunkel asks the question: How could the writer have known what Ahab and Jezebel said to each other in their private chamber?

In Gunkel's perspective, history appeals to our rational instincts, whereas legend cultivates our aesthetic sense.

> *History, which claims to inform us of what has actually happened, is in its very nature prose, while legend is by nature poetry, its aim being to please, to elevate, to inspire, and to move. He who wishes to do justice to such narratives must have some aesthetic faculty, to catch in the telling of a*

*story, what it is and what it purports to be. And in doing so
he is not expressing a hostile or even skeptical judgment,
but simply studying lovingly the nature of his material.
Whoever possesses heart and feeling must perceive, for
instance in the case of the sacrifice of Isaac, that the
important matter is not to establish certain historical facts,
but to impart to the hearer the heartrending grief of the
father who is commanded to sacrifice his child with his own
hand, and then his boundless gratitude and joy when God's
mercy releases him from this grievous trial. And everyone
who perceives the peculiar poetic charm of these old
legends must feel irritated by the barbarian—for there are
pious barbarians—who thinks he is putting the true value
upon these narratives only when he treats them as prose
and history.*[4]

For Gunkel, those who insist on reading all of the Bible as history
demean the qualities of life inherent in story, and for him most of the
book of Genesis is story (saga).

The second half of the 20th century produced considerable discussion on the historical value of the patriarchal narratives. William F. Albright, renowned as an archaeologist, linguist, and historian, sought to show that archaeology would provide a firm base for establishing the history behind the biblical narratives. Several of his students as scholars and teachers promoted this emphasis. Two of them, especially, John Bright and G. Ernest Wright, wrote texts that were widely used in the classroom. Drawing on both the findings of excavations and the vast literature from Egypt and Mesopotamia that had gradually emerged, they argued that, while nothing in particular had been discovered about the patriarchs as such, the names and social patterns were common to the culture of the Middle Bronze Age. Also, the geographical references were demonstrable. On the basis of analogy, the patriarchal narratives could be recognized as having historical validity; at least, this is "the balance of probability."

This movement, known as Biblical Archaeology, dominated the field of Old Testament studies in the 1950s and 1960s. Many of the findings from the numerous excavations, however, both material and literary, bore no apparent relationship to the Bible but took on a life of their own. The motivation for continuing archaeological excavation and the interpretation of this now-extensive field of knowledge gradually began to change. What was developing was a history of the Near East that was independent of the Bible, although biblical studies at points might find information from archaeology useful for interpretation. Consequently, the term Biblical Archaeology was replaced by the term Syro-Palestinian Archaeology, and the field became recognized as an independent discipline. However, this did not diminish the importance of archaeology for constructing a history of Israel. Nevertheless, Albright's expectation that archaeology would confirm the historicity of the biblical narratives has not materialized. In fact, as will be shown, the history behind the narratives is, for the most part, elusive; it is the story, especially the literary and theological character, that makes prominent their appeal.

In what follows, our first task is to learn about the text that we are reading, how it was handed down and what factors contributed to its change or stability. This is, perhaps, the most neglected aspect of the study of the Bible on the part of lay people, and yet what is known about the text has the most profound implications for understanding the place which the Bible holds as the source for cultivating our faith. If we are to search for the text behind the Bible that we read, we should follow the Bible's journey, but in reverse order.

Chapter one notes the most prominent English translations, tracing back the mainstream translation tradition to the 16th century. Since the oldest complete Hebrew Bible is dated in the year 1008, all recent translations are based on this manuscript. Today, with the biblical manuscripts of the Dead Sea Scrolls, which are a thousand years older than the previous established text, we are often faced with the question of which text to translate. This raises the question about the authority of the Bible in relation to a text with uncertainties.

The book of Genesis includes narratives both in the Primeval History (1–11) and the patriarchal legends (12–50) which are well suited to the history-story analysis. For example, the Flood relates closely to Mesopotamian flood stories as well as excavations that have indicated wide-ranging floods. The patriarchs practice customs otherwise known in the Middle Bronze and Late Bronze periods, but anachronisms and duplications suggest something other than history. This is chapter two.

The books of Exodus, Leviticus, and Numbers are treated together in chapter three because there is one major literary unit which binds them together, embracing most of the last half of Exodus, the whole of

Leviticus, and the first 10 chapters of Numbers. It is the Sinai Event, a comprehensive priestly theology. A second binding theme is the journey tradition, which includes several chapters in Exodus and much of the remainder of Numbers. The Exodus story (1–12) is a third theme.

Deuteronomy, a Greek word meaning Second Law, comes from a different source from the books that precede it, except for numerous particular laws in the Code (12–26), which have basic parallels in the Covenant Code of Exodus (20–23), often with differences in application. The book is homiletical in style—a series of sermons attributed to Moses—but it seems to have had a long literary history. Initially, it probably served the early Northern Kingdom and, subsequently, the people of Judah during the reigns of Hezekiah and Josiah. Thus it constitutes chapter four.

Chapter five deals with literature related to the biblical books written during the Intertestamental Period, those books found in the Apocrypha and Pseudepigrapha. Much of this material represents an extension of the biblical writings. The purpose of this chapter is to show how the biblical literature was updated to serve the ongoing interests of the community of Israel. In some cases it was rewritten; in some cases new material was added; in some cases biblical personages were the subject of new developments; in some cases books were written following an established literary pattern or illustrating a moral or theological interest. After describing the books of the Apocrypha and their indeterminate relation to the Old Testament in its history, only the major books of the Pseudepigrapha related to Genesis are selected for discussion, given the limitations due to the volume of material.

The purpose of this book is to provide available information pertinent to understanding the reading of the Old Testament narrative and narrative poetry as history or story. Not that one is more important than the other. They are two different media by which the biblical writers perceived the truth of reality within their grasp. 📖

Notes

1. Israel Finkelstein and Neil Asher Silberman, *The Bible Unearthed* (New York: The Free Press, 2001), 81–82.

2. Hermann Gunkel, *The Legends of Genesis,* trans. W. H. Carruth (New York: Schocken Books, 1964), 4–5.

3. Ibid., 5–6.

4. Ibid., 10–11.

Which Bible?

How can a person, born in today's world, educated in its schools and colleges, ever conscious of its ubiquitous science and technology, read the Bible, not only with understanding but also with appreciation? There is a great gap between the most common life-style and mindset in our time and that common to the ancient Near East out of which the Bible emerged, whether we are talking about the early period of its writing, about a thousand years before Christ, or the completion of the books found in the New Testament by the end of the 3rd century BCE. It is truly amazing that the Bible should have rooted itself so deeply in Western culture and persisted in claiming its appeal in spite of the fact that the gap has gradually grown wider, especially during the past century.

A Heritage of the Church and Synagogue

It is probable that most people who maintain some acquaintance with the Bible do so within the church, for the church has been the institution that has perpetuated the Bible through the centuries. Many hear the Bible read only from the pulpit during worship, a few selected passages intended for exposition. Many others attend church school Bible classes and may use scholarly aids. They discover that as much as they learn, there are always unanswered questions, some of which are very perplexing. Indeed, the few readers who attempt to read the Bible through are those who, if they have the fortitude and persistence to complete the task, are left bewildered as to how it all fits together.

The Bible has always been the treasured tradition of a people. The Christian Bible has its home in the church. In our country, when one wishes to purchase a Bible, not only are there numerous translations from which to choose but some Bibles include the Apocrypha and some do not.

All Christian Bibles have two main parts: the Old Testament and the New Testament. The Old Testament is the Hebrew Bible and, to the Jews, the Bible or the Holy Scriptures. This has its home in the synagogue. The early Christians, who were Greek-speaking, used Greek translations of the Hebrew Scriptures which had been made by Greek-speaking Jews. These included books of the Apocrypha and, sometimes, other books or traditions not included in the Hebrew canon. When the churches of the West underwent a unifying structure with leadership from the Church of Rome, Latin translations emerged based first on Greek translations and then on Hebrew texts by the eminent scholar, Jerome, on assignment from the Pope. Martin Luther, in his translation, followed Jerome in separating the Apocrypha from the Old Testament books, considering the former of lesser value. This became the pattern for the English Bible tradition. Indeed, Protestant reaction against the Apocrypha led to its omission from most English Bibles during the 19th and early 20th centuries.

The New Testament had its beginnings in the early Christian churches where oral traditions about Jesus and letters of Paul circulated. Paul's letters were written during the period 50–70 CE, and the four Gospels which came to be accepted finally with authority were written during the period 60–100 CE. Numerous other Christian writings emerged, some of which were used as Scripture in certain places. Usage served as a sifting process over a period of at least two centuries as the New Testament in its final form took shape.

> *The history of the NT canon, then, was a process extending from the composition of Christian literature in the lst and early 2d centuries, through the spread, use and progressive esteem of these writings in the 2d and 3d centuries, to the determination of a fixed list of authoritative Christian scripture in the 4th and 5th centuries.*[1]

While Jerome translated the Hebrew Bible and the Gospels into Latin at the end of the 4th and beginning of the 5th centuries, there were, from the 2nd and 3rd centuries, translations of all of the biblical books in the Western churches of various regions, which are referred to as

Old Latin texts. By the end of the 8th century, the Latin text was standardized, giving preference to Jerome's translation, in an edition which is known as the Vulgate. The Council of Trent in 1546 made a revision of this text the authoritative Bible of the Roman Catholic Church.[2]

The English Bible

The first English Bibles provoked controversy because they seemed to challenge the authority of the established church. This was the case both with Wycliffe's Bible at the end of the 14th century and the translations of Tyndale in 1525–1536. In an attempt to gain control of the Bible's dissemination while restricting unwanted commentary on it, Henry VIII authorized the Great Bible to be prepared for reading in the churches in 1539. Subsequently, however, he took increasingly restrictive measures to prevent the availability of the Bible. A major change came shortly after Elizabeth, a Protestant, came to the throne in 1558. The Geneva Bible was introduced in England in 1560 and attained such popularity that 140 editions were issued by 1640, remaining the most popular translation for 30 years after the publication of the King James Version.

The King James Version stands as a literary monument for both English Bible translation and English literature. For more than three centuries it was virtually unrivaled in the English speaking world and it remains widely read by conservative Protestants. But language is always changing and hundreds of words in the King James Version are now archaic. Also, its style favors verse by verse assimilation instead of larger literary units with innerconnected thought. However, in recent years, a revision has been made (New King James Version) that improves the readability, making many word substitutions.

The appearance of numerous translations in 16th-century England was due to popular hunger for the Bible and the attempts of the authorities to suppress it. Something similar occurred in the 20th-century English-speaking world in that a spate of translations appeared, particularly since the mid-century. But the motivations behind these versions have been far different. There are three major factors which have initiated these new translations: historical, literary, and theological. First, the discovery of older and better Hebrew and Greek manuscripts along with the enormous fund of new information about the world out of which the Bible emerged has led to the demand for a more "authentic" text. Second, a desire for a more "readable" text has marked all of the new versions. The format demonstrates the paragraph as the major literary unit rather than the verse. Third, most editions include footnotes, introductions, and section headings. Since the churches represent a number of different theological groupings, and every translation is to some degree an interpretation, we find a number of versions that "lean toward" beliefs and practices common to a major theological stance. Thus, the New International Version is, perhaps, most widely read in the conservative, evangelical churches, whereas the Revised Standard Version (or the newer New Revised Standard Version) is the most popular in the mainline Protestant churches. The New American Bible developed within the Roman Catholic Church which it serves. Translations usually give priority to one of two tendencies: following the form of the Hebrew text or capturing the essential meaning whether or not the form can be followed.

The English Bible Lineage

While translations have emerged from a variety of groups for a variety of reasons—for example, Today's English Version, revised as Contemporary English Version, produced by the American Bible Society, emphasizes common parlance—there is a mainstream succession of revisions, each of which was authorized by some recognized authority. The first of these was the Great Bible of 1539, authorized by Henry VIII, who had assumed the position of head of the Church of England. The Bishops Bible (1568), so-called because it was sponsored by the bishops, took the Great Bible as its legitimate predecessor. The King James Version was appointed to be a revision of the Bishops Bible (second edition, 1572), but the primary emphasis on Greek and Hebrew—which had characterized the translation of the popular Geneva Bible—made it somewhat more than a revision. When more ancient manuscripts were discovered well into the 19th century, which necessitated changes in translation, the Church of England authorized a revision. This was published in 1881 and 1885 as the Revised Version. Subsequently, the comparable American Revised Version appeared in 1901. Because of its inferior style, reflecting excessive literalism, the International Council of Religious

Education, which had obtained the copyright, authorized a revision in 1937 and the Revised Standard Version appeared (1946, 1952). A translation of the Apocrypha was added in 1957. To satisfy the Eastern Orthodox churches, three additional texts were added.

> *Thereafter the Revised Standard Version gained the distinction of being officially authorized for use by all major Christian churches: Protestant, Anglican, Roman Catholic, and Eastern Orthodox.*[3]

The Revised Standard Version Bible Committee is a permanent standing committee which assesses critical suggestions and new discoveries. In 1989, a complete revision of the Revised Standard Version was issued called the New Revised Standard Version. Over periods of time, there will always be a need for revisions or new translations.

The following are revisions of the most prominent translations and their predecessors:

‣ **New Revised Standard Version (NRSV),** revision of Revised Standard Version (RSV), revision of American Standard Version (ASV), revision of King James Version (KJV).

‣ **New King James Version (NKJV),** revision of King James Version (KJV).

‣ **Revised English Bible (REB),** revision of New English Bible (NEB).

‣ **New American Standard Version (NASV),** revision of American Standard Version (ASV).

‣ **New Jewish Version (NJV),** revision of Jewish Publication Society Bible (JPS).

The prominent New International Version (NIV), which serves, primarily, the Protestant Evangelical churches, and the New American Bible (NAB), which serves the Roman Catholic Church, are new translations and not revisions.

Bibles Reflect Theological Interests

Study Bibles have become quite popular. A study Bible is a kind of commentary on the Bible. It usually includes general articles about the history of the Bible, the text, the history and geography behind the text, and the literary forms. There is an introduction to each book and foot-notes explaining words, concepts and events, or how a passage relates to other passages. Each major Christian theological group has produced study Bibles reflecting interpretation appropriate to their theology. Among the most prominently available are the following:

Roman Catholic
  ▸ The Catholic Bible, Personal Study Edition
  ▸ New Jerusalem Bible

Protestant Mainline
  ▸ The New Oxford Annotated Bible
  ▸ The Harper Collins Study Bible
  ▸ The Cambridge Annotated Study Bible

Protestant Conservative Evangelical
  ▸ The NIV Study Bible
  ▸ The NKJV Open Bible

Which translation or study Bible do you select to read? It depends on which point of view you wish to adopt. One must first decide whether or not the Apocrypha should be included. Regarding the translation alone, except for the style and the meaning in a few places, the differences are not pronounced. It is in the notations and the comments, which are forms of interpretation, that the differences are notable and a general attitude toward the text is developed. Whichever Bible is selected represents, in some sense, a predetermined point of view as to what the Bible is and what it means.

The Faith Community
and the Scholarly Community

The church, from its beginning, has been the home of the Bible even as the synagogue has been the home of the Hebrew Bible. There has emerged, however, particularly in this and the previous centuries, another home of the Bible, one that is having enormous impact on our knowledge and understanding. In a very loose way, that home can be called the academy but, in our country, it has gradually assumed institutional form in the Society of Biblical Literature (SBL). This professional group, which began in 1880 as a small contingent of college and seminary teachers, has become a learned society of 7,000 members, more than 1,200 of which belong to other countries. Thus, while still strongly American, it is gradually becoming an international organization.

The SBL is devoted to scholarship related to the Bible with emphasis upon philological, literary, historical, and exegetical studies. While some theological interest is represented, it is theology within the Bible or of its historical environs rather than of its subsequent development. Members belong to a multitude of religious organizations or none at all. Of course, the issues that are aired may, and sometimes do, impact theological positions of participants, but where this happens it is usually a by-product of an academic pursuit that, as presented, is searching for objective evidence and logical consistency. Indeed, since the Society is made up largely of academics, presentations are scrutinized with an acumen that dissuades the presenters from exceeding the claims that the evidence allows.

What distinguishes the Society is that, in its annual meetings and the publications of its members, there is represented the leading scholars of all the major religious groups that impute some authority to the Bible: Jews, Roman Catholics, mainline Protestants, and Evangelical Protestants. In addition, there are scholars who do not belong to a faith community. The modern translations of the Bible as well as the study Bibles are the work of academics who relate both to the Society of Biblical Literature and one of the faith communities. In addition, biblical scholars have produced a prodigious quantity of dictionaries, commentaries, and other aids for understanding the Bible as an historical, literary, and theological book. It should be mentioned that two other scholarly societies for the study of the Bible have emerged representing broad faith communities: The Catholic Biblical Association of America and the Evangelical Theological Society.

The present state of the Bible depends on the relationship between the scholarly community and the faith communities. The Bible serves these communities in different ways because they exist for different purposes. However, they are interrelated to the degree that a large number of members of the scholarly community are also members of a faith community. And it appears that it was a strong interest in the Bible gained from the faith community that led these people into the scholarly community.

Members of the faith community consider the Bible to be the primary source that defines their world. For most, the Earth, the solar system, the cosmos go back to a point in time when their existence was initiated by God. Likewise, the human race goes back to a starting point at which the human being either was entirely created by God or was defined as created by the implantation of God's image. But given the developments in the scientific community about cosmic and human origins, there are differences among members of the faith communities as to how they understand theological beginnings. Some, especially in the conservative-evangelical fold, reject evolution and the cosmic time line, favoring a literal interpretation of the creation stories as factual and historical. The liberal-minded, who accept the claims of science, on the other hand, read the stories about origins as parables or myths that tell us who we are in relation to God and the world.

The faith communities use the Bible as a sourcebook for worship, for defining organizational life, for constructing theologies, and for defining the moral life. That there are differences between faith communities in styles and expressions of these endeavors indicates that either they read the Bible differently or they prefer to emphasize certain passages as having priority over other passages. Indeed, it can be said that the authoritative documents of each Christian denomination reflect a canon within the canon, that is, a selection of biblical passages that support a harmoniously rational belief system and an order for both corporate and personal Christian practice. But the Bible is seen as the sourcebook for cultivating human life as it ought to be and for providing a comprehensive meaning for our lives. That most faith communities consider the Bible to be in some sense the Word of God means that the God who is revealed in the Bible deserves their ultimate commitment.

The enormous amount of activity related to biblical studies on the part of the scholarly community has placed the Bible in a kind of transitional stage of development that, as far as we can see, may continue indefinitely. Gone is that long period when the King James Version reigned as an unchanging document, unfazed by the vicissitudes of common culture. To say that the Bible is in a stage of development may need some explanation. Not that the canon is open or is about to be opened, although there is some movement in that direction, but we can no longer think of the Bible as an isolated text apart from what has become an incredibly large historical world out of which it has emerged. That world is ever impinging on the biblical text in new ways. In the last half-century a great fund of new documents from the biblical world, many of which are biblical, are requiring a fresh examination of the text as we have known it. Although in recent translations, the changes may be small, there is much discussion of Jesus' sayings in the apocryphal Gospel of Thomas, which have many parallels to the canonical gospels, regarding its authenticity. Also, there are biblical scrolls among the Dead Sea Scrolls that are substantially different from the text that has served as the major source for modern translations. The ongoing study of this material does, indeed, constitute a stage in the development of the Bible. We can be confident that, for the most part, the Bible will remain basically the same, but some of the text will undoubtedly undergo changes of lesser or greater magnitude in the coming years. And there may be passages where translators will provide alternate versions based on ancient textual traditions that merit equal consideration, as is found to a limited extent in the footnotes of some recent translations.

The Hebrew Text Behind the Old Testament and the Septuagint

How did our Bible come to us? What are the sources available today from which translations are made? Here it is necessary to distinguish between the Old and New Testaments before the period of the 16th-century English translations, when the Hebrew and Greek testaments became the major sources instead of the Latin. Up to this time, the Hebrew Bible had been transmitted entirely within the Jewish community, whereas the Greek New Testament had come down through the Christian Church. It was the burgeoning interest in the Bible sparked by the Reformation that led translators back to its roots.

The early English translations of the Old Testament were based on late medieval Hebrew copies. We must remember that prior to the advent of printing in the mid-15th century all copies were transcribed by hand. While Jewish scribes had achieved a remarkable degree of accuracy in copying the Hebrew Bible, differences appear between copies. The text of the early printed Hebrew Bibles is eclectic, the editors having used a selection of handwritten copies as a base. Recent English translations are based, primarily, on a single manuscript, the so-called Leningrad Codex dated 1008, the oldest complete

Hebrew Bible. A somewhat earlier Aleppo Codex, lacking the Torah and a few other books, is being prepared for publication and may serve as the primary text for future translations. But even this dates more than a thousand years after the completion of the writing of the Old Testament.

It has been the task of textual criticism, which had become a major discipline through the first half of the 20th century, to find the earliest witnesses to the text. Prior to the discovery of the Dead Sea Scrolls, the oldest manuscripts were Greek translations of the Old Testament known as the Septuagint, dating from the 4th and 5th centuries CE. These manuscripts are thought to contain a collection of translated books from different sources because they show a lack of uniformity in relation to the medieval Hebrew text. Some books reflect that Hebrew almost literally while others vary considerably. The Septuagint Book of Jeremiah, for example, is about one-sixth shorter than the Masoretic Text.

The Masoretic Text, represented by the medieval manuscripts, received its name from the Jewish scholars of the Middle Ages known as Masoretes. After the destruction of the Temple and of Jerusalem in 70 CE the Jews as a community had only their traditions left. As People of the Book, every attempt was made to preserve their sacred writings. The Torah and the Prophets had long since been given authoritative status, but it was necessary to decide which other books deserved to be canonized. From Jewish tradition and from Josephus, it appears as if the discussion of which books "defile the hands" (are sacred) had gone on among the Rabbis throughout the Intertestamental Period.[4] At what point agreement was reached within the Jewish community is hard to say, since extant Hebrew Bibles are not earlier than the 10th century.

The Masoretes were the guardians of the text. It was their task to add whatever was necessary to the text to secure its preservation, pronunciation, and intonation. The fact is that up until their time, only the consonants of the words were written down, often with the use of one of four consonants to indicate a vowel. The oral rendering of the text was simply passed on orally. Thus, during the period of about 500–900 CE, they devised written systems of vocalization and intonation that they added to the consonantal text. They also compiled an enormous quantity of statistics about the text and made marginal comments where they perceived textual problems.

Other Early Witnesses to the Hebrew Text

In addition to the Masoretic Text and the Septuagint as witnesses to "the Text," translators have:

▸ **The Samaritan Pentateuch**—a parallel to the Hebrew text in Samaritan script. While the available manuscript copies are Medieval, they represent an independent tradition that goes back to the pre-Christian centuries through the Samaritan community, which still exists on Mt. Gerizim. This is now comfirmed by the Dead Sea Scrolls. Comparison with the Masoretic Text indicates about 6,000 differences, mostly orthographic (variations in spelling), but about 1,900 of them show agreement with the Septuagint instead of the Masoretic Text.[5]

▸ **Aramaic Targums**—These are Aramaic renderings: sometimes translation, sometimes paraphrase, sometimes commentary, the texts of which derive from the Middle Ages but the traditions of which go back to the pre-Christian centuries. Some targums were found among the Dead Sea Scrolls.

▸ **The Peshitta**—the Syriac translation, some manuscripts of which go back to the 5th century CE.

▸ **Latin Bibles**—about 8,000 manuscripts exist from the Middle Ages. The oldest complete Latin Bible comes from the beginning of the 8th century.[6]

The Dead Sea Scrolls

The discovery of the Dead Sea Scrolls represents a landmark in our understanding of the Old Testament, the importance of which can hardly be overestimated. They consist of thousands of fragments of hundreds of scrolls as well as some that are complete or nearly complete. There are at least 175 scrolls of biblical books represented, not counting the Apocrypha. Seventy of these are of the Pentateuch (Torah). Every book of the Old Testament is represented except Esther and Nehemiah, although Nehemiah would have been found on the same scroll with Ezra, and only one scroll with Ezra material has been found.[7] Most of the material, including the more complete scrolls, has been published, and it is now possible to draw some conclusions about the text of these biblical scrolls in relation to the Masoretic Text that stands behind our current translations.

First, it must be said that we do not know if there was an idea of "canon" in the Qumran community where the scrolls were found. There is no evidence for one. The scrolls that were found are diverse in character. There are scrolls of community life and structure, poems and liturgies, biblical commentaries, horoscopes, texts of Old Testament books, Apocrypha, Pseudepigrapha, and others, about 800 in all. Some scrolls are written in Aramaic, a few in Greek. No part of the New Testament text has been found. If the number of scrolls that were found of each biblical book is any indication of their relative importance to the Qumran community, we can list the following recent count of the most numerous.

1. Psalms—34 scrolls*
2. Deuteronomy—27 scrolls
3. Isaiah—20–24 scrolls
4. Genesis—19–20 scrolls
5. Exodus—14–16 scrolls
6. Leviticus—9 scrolls
7. 12 minor prophets—8 scrolls
8. Daniel—8 scrolls [8]

As noted below, Peter Flint, a specialist on this topic, identifies 36 psalms scrolls from Qumran.

It is notable that fragments of 12 scrolls of the Book of Jubilees and 11 Aramaic scrolls of the Book Enoch were found.[9] These books belong to what is called the Pseudepigrapha.

Another factor associated with the idea of "canon" is the form in which it appears. When we use the word "Bible" it is a single entity, a book between the covers of which all canonical material is found. The Dead Sea Scrolls were written before the codex—or book form—was invented.

There was no union of biblical books except as they were grouped together on a single scroll, as were the 12 minor prophets and Ezra-Nehemiah. Indeed, when we observe that the four scrolls of the Latter Prophets—Isaiah, Jeremiah, Ezekiel, and the 12—are similar in length, perhaps about as long as a scroll can be for practical purposes, we must allow that practical limitation was a factor in determining what and how much was written. As we shall see, there was a tendency for traditions to grow over a period of many generations.

It is the content of the scrolls that is particularly enlightening. In comparing the text of scrolls of the same biblical book there is often variety: variety in the wording, variety in specific content of given sections whereby some are longer than others, and variety in the arrangement of the material. It is not uncommon to find "new" material in a scroll of a biblical book that is not found in our Bibles.

Redefining the Text for Translation

I have noted that the Old Testament text in our Bibles is based primarily on the Hebrew Masoretic Text, the tradition of the Masoretes which they edited and refined from about 100 CE to about 1000 CE. But we have also noted that there are two other major textual traditions that are independent of the Masoretic tradition and that go back to the period considerably before the destruction of Jerusalem and the Temple in 70 CE, namely, the Septuagint and the Samaritan Pentateuch. What the Qumran biblical texts now show is that all three of these traditions are represented in the scrolls and, further, that many of the scrolls at points may represent features of one, two, or all three of these traditions or may indicate an independence of all three of them. "The Qumran evidence has . . . established that diverse forms of the Heb text were current down to the 1st century CE."[10]

In the New Revised Standard Version, at the end of chapter 10 of I Samuel, there is a paragraph of four sentences which, until recently, has never before appeared in an English Bible. Except for the very beginning and ending, it is missing from the Masoretic Text. It is found in one of the scrolls and, as the footnote explains, it was known by Josephus. Also, at the beginning of chapter 11 there is a phrase, "About a month later," which again is new to our English Bible text. It is from the same scroll but is also found in the Septuagint. This phrase binds the two chapters together.

As one examines the footnotes of the NRSV version of the Books of Samuel, there are numerous examples where the translators have preferred the texts of the scrolls and the Septuagint to the Masoretic Text. Actually, the differences between these textual traditions are much more extensive than these footnotes show. One authority has characterized the Masoretic Samuel as follows:

> *The received Hebrew text of Samuel in its Masoretic dress*
> *(MT) is in poor repair. It is a short text, but its shortness is*
> *not the wholesome shortness of a text free of expansion and*
> *interpolation; rather it is the result of countless copying*
> *errors and omissions, some of them extensive, scattered*
> *throughout the book.*[11]

Translators have developed methods and principles by which to evaluate and compare texts. Often they are able to detect errors in transmission and to discern the superior of two or more texts. But there are times when two parallel texts can claim equal validity.[12]

Two Text-Witnesses to Jeremiah

It has long been known that the Septuagint version of the Book of Jeremiah is strikingly different from the Masoretic Text. It is one-eighth to one-sixth shorter, depending on which scholar is counting, lacking words, phrases, whole sentences, and entire sections found in the Masoretic Text.[13] There are numerous differences in the arrangement of the text, most notably the section known as Oracles Against the Nations, which in Greek is chapters 26–32 and in the Masoretic Text is chapters 46–51. Until the discovery of the Dead Sea Scrolls, it was not possible to evaluate the relation between these two textual traditions with confidence. But now portions of Hebrew scrolls have been found—at least two of each—which support both text types. Both the longer and the shorter texts of the Book of Jeremiah were in circulation in the Qumran community.

One of the most respected scholars of the text, Emanuel Tov, has advanced the theory that these two textual traditions represent two different editions of the Book of Jeremiah. The Septuagint version is a translation of the first Hebrew edition and the Masoretic Text is the second edition which, Tov argues, is post-exilic.

> *In edition II changes were inserted in the order of the*
> *verses and in wording, but more frequently elements were*
> *added: sections now occurring twice (e.g. 8:10b–12 for*
> *which cf. 6:13–15; 17:3–4, cf. 15:13–14; 30:10–11, cf.*
> *46:27–28); new verses and sections (the largest ones are*
> *33:14–26 and 51:44b–49a); new details; brief*

explanations, in particular, expansions of proper nouns; expansions on the basis of the context; expansions of formulae, etc.[14]

Whether or not Tov is correct that the two texts in hand represent two editions, the scholarly community now considers the Greek version to be a witness to the earlier and more authentic form.

The developing consensus of scholarship now is that the shorter text on which G* (the original Greek text) is based represents the more original and superior textual tradition of the book of Jeremiah.[15]

This evaluation poses a fundamental question for the future. Will new translations of the Bible into English prefer the Septuagint version of the Book of Jeremiah and the Dead Sea Scrolls that support it instead of the Masoretic Text, which up until now has served as the basis for all English translations? It would follow the established principle of translating the earlier and more authentic text, but would play havoc with the chapter and verse structure so ingrained in the English Bible tradition. The faithful in the church and synagogue have adapted to minor changes in the text as new translations have appeared, but this would represent a radical change in content. Perhaps one should expect both textual traditions to be represented in different translations to serve the public interest. This would replicate what was available in the Qumran community.

An Exodus Scroll

Judith Sanderson, one of the scholars assigned to examine the scrolls, has made a detailed study of an Exodus scroll from cave 4. She has identified it as having a text type of the Samaritan Pentateuch. There are major expansions to the text: (a) repetitions, especially in the plague narratives; (b) inserts into the text from other places in Exodus; (c) four passages inserted from the Book of Deuteronomy; and (d) sectarian readings common to the Samaritan Pentateuch. There are also omissions and other alterations in the text. Sanderson concludes that scribes were not slavish copyists at this time but exercised some decision making in editing the text.

> *The major expansions show that some scribes in this period*
> *felt the freedom to add liberally to the biblical text for literary*
> *purposes, such as filling out the narrative or creating greater*
> *harmony with a parallel in another part of Exodus or in*
> *Deuteronomy, or for theological and perhaps political*
> *purposes, such as magnifying the glory of Yahweh, either in*
> *opposition to the sinfulness of the people or in support of the*
> *mediatorship of Moses or a prophet like him.*

She notes, however, that the editing was restricted to text in the scrolls. "No new text was added."[16]

One of the most eminent scholars of the Dead Sea Scrolls, Shemaryahu Talmon, has observed this scribal phenomenon as common to the era.

> *It may be said that in ancient Israel, and probably also in*
> *other ancient Near Eastern cultures, especially in*
> *Mesopotamia, the professional scribe seldom if ever was*
> *merely a slavish copyist of the material which he handled.*
> *He rather should be considered a minor partner in the*
> *creative literary process. To a degree, he applied on the*
> *reproductive level norms and techniques which had*
> *informed his predecessors, the ancient authors, and which*
> *had become his literary legacy. The right to introduce*
> *variations into the biblical text, within limits, had come to*
> *the Bible-oriented copyists and quoting authors of post-*
> *biblical works, together with the transmitted writings.*
> *Mechanical faithfulness to the letter of the sanctified*
> *traditional literature is to become the rule only after the*
> *undirected and intuitive process of canonization had*
> *completed its course, i.e., not earlier than the first century*
> *BCE and not later than the second century CE.*[17]

The Psalms Scrolls

Peter Flint has made a meticulous study of all of the Psalms scrolls. There are 36 from Qumran and three from other sites, making a total of 39. They range in size and content from a few fragments to a scroll that is about 5 meters long and preserves 49 compositions known as 11QPs[a] (11 for cave 11, Q for Qumran, Ps for Psalms and "a" to distinguish it from other Psalms scrolls found in the same cave). Of the 49 items, 39 are psalms found in Books IV and V of the Masoretic Psalter (90–150), although not always in the same arrangement. Of the other 10 items, one is known as "David's Last Words" found in II Samuel 23:1–7; "five were familiar from ancient translations, Psalms 154 and 155 (in Syriac); Ps. 151A, Ps 151B and Sirach 51:13–30 (in Greek, Syriac, and Latin), and four were completely unknown."[18]

A major general observation emerges from Flint's study, namely, the fluidity of the text. There are three different manifestations of this fluidity. First, Flint lists hundreds of variants, a variant being a reading in a scroll, other than orthographic, which differs from either another scroll or the Masoretic Text. Second, the arrangement of the psalms differs in 60 percent of cases from that of the Masoretic Text in Books IV and V (90–150). For Books I–III (1–89), there are scrolls which preserve 42 cases of adjoining psalms and these follow the order of the Masoretic Text in all but four instances. Third, as already noted in 11QPsª, compositions other than the MT Psalms are sometimes included.

Flint supports the conclusion, which James Sanders drew in his earlier study of 11QPsª, that it served as a "true scriptural Psalter" at Qumran. But he differs from Sanders regarding the stabilization process. "This stabilization took place not gradually, but in two distinct stages: Psalms 1–89 (or thereabouts) prior to the 1st century BCE, and Psalms 90 onwards towards the end of the 1st century CE."[19] For the second section of the Psalms, Flint assumes two different editions.

The Psalms scrolls preserve at least three literary editions of the Psalter: Edition I (Psalms 1/2-89), Edition IIa or the 11QPsª-Psalter (=Edition I plus the arrangement found in 11QPsª), and Edition IIb or the MT-150 (=Edition I plus Psalms 90-150).[20]

As with the textual tradition of Jeremiah, the same fundamental question applies to the Psalms. Which text of the Psalms should we prefer? The collection of Psalms 2–89 seems to have attained a fixed arrangement for the Jewish community as a whole since it is common (with very few exceptions) to the Dead Sea Scrolls, the Septuagint, and the Masoretic Text. Psalm 1 may be a later addition because Psalm 2— the most quoted Psalm in the New Testament—is referred to as Psalm 1 in several manuscripts of Acts 13:33. Flint notes, however, that a large number of variants in the Psalms scrolls of this collection agree with the Septuagint version rather than the Masoretic Text.[21] While differences among witnesses are often resolved by principles of textual criticism, there are variants where different readings seem of equal merit. Where this is the case, editors should not decide which reading is placed in the text and which is relegated to a footnote. Both can be placed in the text in parentheses. The reading public deserves the right to see the ambiguities in the textual tradition.

Which Text Do We Translate?

More importantly, this fundamental question applies to the choice of collections. We must recognize that our adoption of the Masoretic Text, which is the basis for the Protestant English Bible tradition, is a confirmation of the decisions made by the leadership of the mainline Jewish community from about 100 CE to about 1000 CE. These decisions apply to the selection of books to be canonized for the third section of the canon, since the authority of the Law and the Prophets had long since been established. However, it was not only the selection of the books but of the editions of the books which were to be included. And, over the centuries, the vocalization of the consonantal text crystalized the very specific form of the text that has come down to us.

While the differences between the Masoretic Text and the Septuagint, on the one hand, and the Samaritan Pentateuch, on the other hand, have long been recognized, the Hebrew manuscripts of the Dead Sea Scrolls, which support all three of these textual traditions, now present a new situation regarding the text to be translated. We can no longer assume that the Masoretic Text is the norm against which the other textual traditions are to be evaluated. Texts deserve to be compared and the principles of textual criticism applied, but often different readings of parallel texts should be presented for all to see. When asked what a passage of the Bible says, in many cases the honest answer is that one tradition says one thing and that another tradition says something else.

Conclusion

I have surveyed the text of the Old Testament based on extant manuscripts. I have found evidence for a fluid tradition prior to the 2nd century CE. From then until about 1000 CE, the rabbis made an intense collective effort to solidify the tradition into a singular text that could not be changed. The invention of the printing press further consolidated the text. This is the text used by the translators of the English versions, early and recent, the so-called Masoretic Text.

The early English translations faced a problematic existence because they threatened ecclesiastic authority. King James I, however, initiated a translation that came to be known as the Authorized Version, which, for about three centuries in the Protestant English speaking world, assumed an uncontested authority not unlike that of the Masoretic Text.

During the last one and a half centuries, a number of developments have emerged to radically alter our view of the biblical text. Most significantly, the Dead Sea Scrolls are having a phenomenal impact in revealing multifarious readings in manuscripts that are 1,000 years earlier than the Leningrad manuscript. The scrolls are also giving increasing credibility to the Septuagint and the Samaritan Pentateuch. What has emerged is a collection of diverse renderings of biblical books and related materials that challenge the view of the Bible as a singular entity. For the Old Testament, we are left with the question: Which textual tradition do we adopt? 📖

1. Harry Y. Gamble, "Canon" in *Anchor Bible Dictionary,* ed. David Noel Freedman (New York: Doubleday, 1992), 1:853.

2. D. C. Parker, "Vulgate" in *Anchor Bible Dictionary,* 6:860–61.

3. Bruce M. Metzger, "Preface" in *The New Oxford Annotated Bible,* ed. Bruce M. Metzger and Roland E. Murphy (New York: Oxford University Press, 1991), x.

4. G. W. Anderson, "Canonical and Non-Canonical" in *The Cambridge History of the Bible,* ed. P. R. Ackroyd and C. F. Evans (Cambridge: Cambridge University Press, 1970), 1:114–18.

5. Ernst Wuerthwein, *The Text of the Old Testament,* trans. Erroll F. Rhodes (Grand Rapids: William B. Eerdmans Publishing Co., 1979), 42–43.

6. J. Gribomont, "Latin Versions" in *The Interpreter's Dictionary of the Bible,* ed. Keith Crim (Nashville: Abingdon, 1976), Supplementary Volume: 531.

7. Geza Vermes, *The Dead Sea Scrolls* (Philadelphia: Fortress Press, 1977), 198–209.

8. Emanuel Tov, *Textual Criticism of the Hebrew Bible* (Minneapolis: Augsburg Fortress, 2001), 104–05.

9. Vermes, *Dead Sea Scrolls,* 210.

10. John J. Collins, "Dead Sea Scrolls" in *Anchor Bible Dictionary,* 2:89.

11. R. Kyle McCarter, Jr., *The Anchor Bible, vol. 8, I Samuel* (New York: Doubleday, 1980), 5.

12. See, for example, M. Tsevat's discussion of I Samuel 14:41 in "Samuel, I and II," in *The Interpreter's Dictionary of the Bible,* Supplementary Volume: 778.

13. Tov, *Textual Criticism,* 320.

14. Tov, 321.

15. Robert P. Carroll, *Jeremiah* (Philadelphia: Westminster Press, 1986), 51.

16. Judith E. Sanderson, *An Exodus Scroll From Qumran* (Atlanta: Scholars Press, 1986), 299.

17. Frank Moore Cross and Shemaryahu Talmon, *Qumran and the History of the Biblical Text* (Cambridge: Cambridge University Press, 1976), 381.

18. Peter W. Flint, *The Dead Sea Psalms Scrolls and the Book of Psalms* (Leiden: Brill, 1997), 40.

19. Ibid., 148.

20. Ibid., 227.

21. Ibid., 231–32.

Genesis

Is the Old Testament a history book or a storybook? On the one hand, it has all the markings of a comprehensive history. From the Mesopotamian migrant family which led to the Hebrew tribes, the first half of the Old Testament, Genesis through Esther—in all but Jewish Bibles, which have a different arrangement—is descriptive of Israel's ongoing experience in community and provides an extensive genealogical profile of its leadership well into the post-exilic period. Coupled with the New Testament, it goes from the beginning of time to the end of time. It begins with the creation of the world and ends with the consummation of all things in heaven and on Earth, a new creation beyond time.

The Old Testament Narrative
Presented as History

In its preface, Genesis 1–11, this framework presents the unfolding of the natural world and then the human world in the ancient Near East. In the space of a few chapters, in stark reserve, the first humans develop into the peoples of the ancient Near East. Out of this context, in somewhat bolder format, the Patriarchs, in family line, reveal the cultural and geographical world of the land of Canaan and the ever-present consciousness of the God who calls them, guides them, and sustains them. The sons of Jacob become tribes in Egypt and these tribes become an amalgamated Israel under the leadership of Moses.

The Lord delivers Israel from the oppression of the Egyptians. Moses leads them into the wilderness, where the community undergoes its spiritual formation as found in the books of Exodus, Leviticus, Numbers, and Deuteronomy. Laws are given: for devotional religious practice, for proper family and community relationships, for the care of property in the land that is soon to be occupied, for escaping the depravity of foreign peoples and their religion.

The Book of Joshua in two equal parts (1–12, 13–24) describes the rapid, devastating, and complete conquest of the land of Canaan and the distribution of the land to the tribes. Judges portrays the cycle of apostasy, repentance, and deliverance in one tribe after the other, the judges being heroic leaders contending with the indigenous peoples of Canaan. There is no authority binding the tribes, and the book ends with civil war.

Samuel, the prophet-priest, exercises intertribal leadership and appoints a king, Saul, for the necessary defense against the well-organized Philistines. This is the beginning of Israel as a state and, while Saul falters because of ambivalent public support, and because he is rejected by Samuel, a military climate develops which fosters organization and skills that bring victory and acclaim to the talented David, the next king. Under him, Israel subdues all other Canaanite peoples and becomes a highly organized state during his and the following generation. King Solomon, David's son, exercises tyrannical rule in his attempt to build a kingdom of splendor, demanding so much in taxes and state labor that the citizenry rebels and the 10 northern tribes secede, forming their own kingdom.

As the Books of Samuel deal largely with the formation of the United Monarchy, the Books of Kings present its demise and the ongoing kingships of what came to be known as the Kingdom of Judah in the south and the Kingdom of Israel in the north. The latter is taken over by the Assyrians in 722 BCE and those tribes become lost to further biblical record. Judah survives until the Babylonian destruction of Jerusalem and of the Temple in 586 BCE, after which its leadership class is taken into exile to Babylon. This is the end of the Judean kingdom.

The Books of Chronicles parallel, and apparently borrow from and modify, much of II Samuel and the Books of Kings but with a decidedly Levitical and priestly emphasis. The extensive material on the prophets is omitted, as is all other reference to the Kingdom of Israel except when it relates to the Kingdom of Judah. The first nine chapters are a lengthy genealogy from Adam to well into the post-exilic period.

The end of Chronicles duplicates the beginning of Ezra, which with Nehemiah represents a collection of reports about the return of the Jews from Babylon to Jerusalem and life in the community over an extended period of time. Esther tells of the plot in the Persian court to eliminate the Jews and Queen Esther's successful efforts to thwart it.

This is a brief summary of the first half of the Old Testament, the primary narrative, which describes the origin of the people of Israel, their life in community in the land of Canaan, their struggles, fortunes, and misfortunes, recounting generation after generation with genealogical lists and kingly succession. It purports to be an historical narrative.

The Primeval History Read As Story

On the other hand, the Old Testament gives the appearance of a storybook. It even begins with what may be read as story language.

> *When God began to create the heaven and the earth—the earth being unformed and void, with darkness over the surface of the deep and a wind from God sweeping over the water—God said, 'Let there be light;' and there was light.*

This is the way the New Jewish Version translates it. The way we read depends to some degree on what we bring to what we read. The same text read as history or story produces two quite different meanings. Actually, the first literary unit, Genesis 1:1–2:4a, is in the form of a liturgy. Throughout, there is statement and response, the response representing the fulfillment of the statement: "And God said. . . . And it was so." Liturgy is a form of communal expression, a communal expression of faith. The content of this story does not stem from historical observation. It derives from tested intuition, the perception of the world in its broadest sense against the backdrop of an ill-conceived polytheistic worldview. It says that the God of Israel's faith, in His singular glory, is the sole creative power of everything that can be conceived. The belief in creation, as expressed in the biblical stories, rests on spiritual comprehension. It does not, as in science, derive from measurement and classification. Revelation is an interior experience, a persistent indelible insight. There is no conflict between the biblical view of creation and the scientific theory of the origin of the universe. God creates by His Word, which defines the region of experience designated as God's world. It is not a material world, although the material world is influenced by it. God's motivating force induces humans to manipulate the mundane world by divine direction.

History presents what was; story, at least biblical story, presents what is, or what is in what was. The first story of creation is not a record of what happened. It is a representation of God's sovereignty over all the world, of the dignity inherent in human beings, and of the celebration of the sacred. It is faith language. To think of this as history, as some still do, is to be blind to the functions of literature.

The Garden of Eden is a second story of creation but a far different one. Whereas Genesis 1 is cosmic and universal, commanding and awesome, the Genesis 2–3 story is local, social, intimate, and didactic. The first displays the transcendence of God, the second God's immanence. The Garden of Eden is a story in the more traditional sense. It begins and ends as we expect a story to do. It has a plot and characters, exposes motivations and actions. There is a villain, the talking serpent, and the plot plays out with dire consequences. Later generations have known implicitly that this represents the human story.

All of the stories of the Primeval History, Genesis 1–11, are both universal in scope and basic for setting the stage for telling the story of Israel. The Flood (Genesis 6:5–9:19) provides the means of establishing a new beginning. The Lord is said to bring the Flood to blot out human wickedness. Of course, all the animals perish also, all but those that are saved by Noah in the Ark, which are designated as clean and unclean, a distinction which is applicable to Israel's manner of life. So we see cultic distinctions, undoubtedly active at the time of the writing, being superimposed on a mythical primeval story. The Flood also serves the purpose of eliminating the knowledge of everything that came before. This is God's new beginning with Noah, a righteous man who sacrifices to the Lord with clean animals. Nations emerge from the descendants of Noah defining the broader political world known to Israel.

It should be obvious that this is not history but a story, although at least one expedition has gone looking for the Ark. The idea of harboring pairs of all the animals in the Ark is so unrealistic as to be the stuff of comedy, and if a flood covered the whole Earth, anyone digging anywhere would find a deep layer of silt. It is as story that the Flood has such profound meaning, the judgment of God blotting out wickedness and establishing a human community based on righteousness. Indeed, new beginnings are characteristic of the biblical story.

The Tower of Babel is both an etiological story and a second story of the Fall. Coming after the Table of Nations in chapter 10, the editors needed an explanation for the multitude of languages spoken throughout these nations. Since these nations were all said to be descendants of Noah, a righteous man, a further explanation was needed to show how the reality of depravity came to exist, since the other descendants of Adam had all theoretically been wiped out. Human ingenuity builds towers that elevate names. To make a name for oneself is the evidence of pride. This story form, characteristic of myth, is evident by the opening words of the narrative: "Now the whole earth had one language."

There are a few other brief stories in the Primeval History: Cain and Abel, a story of acceptance and rejection, of rivalry, murder, and punishment; the founders of primitive culture—the author apparently didn't know that the smelting of iron didn't occur until about 1200 BCE, for him it was way back there; the sons of God begetting children with human women, accounting for a group of unusually large people known as the Nephilim; and the curse of Canaan, attributed to his having seen the drunken Noah's nakedness. These stories serve to explain conditions and consequences in the ongoing experience of the Israelite community rather than reporting the past. They speak to perennial questions about how some things came to be as they are through mythic tradition.

From the very beginning, there is throughout the Bible an ever-present vertical dimension which is spatial in character yet intrinsically moral. In the Bible's opening statement where the New Jewish Version translates "a wind from God", as noted above, an equally valid translation is "the Spirit of God," as found in the traditional versions. The Hebrew word means wind, breath, or spirit. However, the phrase used here is found nearly a hundred times in the Hebrew Bible meaning "the Spirit of God." God hovers over the world and over the whole historical process. There is initially and with remarkable conciseness a setting in which God brings the cosmos into being, and establishes celestial movement, life forms, and the peopling of nations. With the dramatic descriptive examples of the Garden of Eden, Cain and Abel, the Flood, and the Tower of Babel, the moral—or, rather, immoral—condition of human beings is exposed and punitive action is meted out. Yet out of the unremitting judgment, God provides some redemption, the major example being Noah, who inaugurates a new beginning. This theological pattern repeats itself several times in the ongoing biblical story.

In the interest of brevity regarding the distant past, which serves as a prelude to the biblical story, the writers employed the device of genealogy. This is the means of establishing the idea of history through continuity, and the extraordinary life spans attributed to the forefathers telescopes the early veiled eon, bringing it down to a stage that represents the more immediate setting for the history of Israel, which is the biblical story.

The Israelite writers who depicted this earliest period, commonly called the Primeval History, borrowed from the traditions of the peoples of Mesopotamia and adapted them to their own theological perspective. Some of the names of the antediluvian patriarchs are similar to those of the king lists of the Sumerians. And while it is commonly thought that Methuselah is the oldest person on record, the life spans of those kings are said to be between 18,000 and 65,000 years.[1] Genealogies of ancient ancestral figures of such heroic proportions, therefore, seem to indicate the period of the lengthy but unknown past.

It is instructive to note that the ages of the 10 antediluvian patriarchs (Adam to Noah; there are also 10 in Babylonian tradition) are between 900 and 1,000 years; those Mesopotamian patriarchs after the Flood (Shem to Terah) are assigned 200 to 600 years; the ancestors of the people of Israel who lived in Canaan and Egypt (Abram to Joseph) are said to be 100 to 200 years in age. Finally, the normal expected human life span is given in later tradition as 70 years (Psalm 90:10).

There is a remarkable change of focus in reading the Bible as soon as historical information from the outside enters the picture. It sometimes comes as an intrusion. Taken alone, the early chapters of the Bible seem to reflect an archaic world that is so distant in its past that it doesn't belong to present reality. It takes on the character of a fantasy world. Those unrealistic life spans, the talking serpent in the Garden of Eden, the flood that covered the whole Earth—these belong to the sense of stories rather than that of history.

The Story of the Flood

There are, however, some points of connection with life on Earth and with more ancient tradition in these stories. The story of the Flood (Genesis 6–9) takes on a different perspective in light of information from Mesopotamia dug up by archaeologists. Archaeology is a strict science. It uses the methods common to the sciences in digging ancient mounds in the regions of locations mentioned in the Bible. It does not attempt to prove anything but to provide information, which may have some bearing on statements in the Bible or life in general in biblical times. When that information is interpreted in relation to the Bible, it is no longer the function of archaeology, strictly speaking, but of the broader subject of history. Whereas archaeology is a branch of history, it is the scientific branch and seeks to be objective in its findings. History, insofar as it is interpretation, is subjective, but it is not always easy to draw the line between fact and interpretation.

No evidence for a flood has been found in any excavation in Palestine. Excavations in Mesopotamia at several sites, however, have found layers of silt, some very deep. In the 1920s and 30s, Sir Leonard Woolley, an archaeologist of repute, digging at Ur in lower Mesopotamia near the Euphrates River, found a level of silt 10 feet deep dated in the middle of the 4th millennium BCE. But in two other sites near the Euphrates where Woolley dug, one 4 miles away and the other 40 miles upstream, no silt was found. Then again, at the ancient city of Kish, nearly 200 miles upstream, a flood level was found, but it belongs to the 3rd millennium. It cannot relate to the flood at Ur. It should be noted, also, that cultural remains both before and after the flood at Ur point to the same civilization. Flood levels from different periods were found at the ancient city of Nineveh along the Tigris River, hundreds of miles northwest of Ur.[2] The evidence from these sites indicates that there were inundations of great magnitude which must have wreaked enormous devastation, but they were local or regional in their extent.

Archaeologists sometimes uncover written materials, even at times whole libraries. Such was the case at Nineveh with the discovery of the library of the 7th century BCE Assyrian monarch, Ashurbanipal. Among the thousands of clay tablets was the Epic of Gilgamesh, a mythic heroic figure. The 11th tablet of this epic includes a story of the Flood with remarkable parallels to the Genesis story. The gods decide to inundate the Earth, but one of them informs a figure comparable to Noah and counsels him to build an ark to save his family and the animals. The flood comes, three birds are sent out in sequence, and the ship comes to rest on a mountain. Sacrifices are offered.

Several other versions of this story have been found, as early as the Sumerians and as late as the Greeks. With some common features and some modifications, it appears that there was a common flood tradition from early times throughout Mesopotamia and beyond. The Noah story derives from that tradition. However, the theological interpretation is unique and strikingly different. The flood tradition provided a model by which the relation between God and humans could be expressed.

The Genesis story of the Flood illustrates a methodology used by the religious writers in ancient Israel to express the character of God. There is good reason to believe that traditions circulated commonly in ancient societies. Since writing materials were scarce and expensive, it is likely that, except in the professional circles of the court and cultic religious circles, particularly prophets, priests, and wise men, oral tradition was the means of circulation. Intercultural tradition followed intercultural travel. The keepers of the faith in the Israelite religious circles confronted traditions of other cultures by transforming them. The God of Israel supplanted the gods of the nations. The Flood was interpreted as the instrument of God's judgment against perversity and decadence. Noah became the agent of a new start leading to a new community, the life of which was to be defined by the God of Israel. The traditions of the nations were not rejected; they were reconstructed to become vessels of legitimate theology. Modern scholars have observed two versions of the Noah story that have been integrated into one. They come from two different cultic circles in ancient Israel, one from the 10th or 9th century BCE, the other from the 6th century BCE. The earlier one is said to come from the Yahwist, whose traditions about early Israel are found throughout Genesis, Exodus, and Numbers. The later one, more ritualistic in emphasis, is known as the Priestly writer, and is found throughout the first four books.

The Story of Creation

Also found in the library at Nineveh, as well as in several other sites in Mesopotamia, was what is now known as the Babylonian story of creation, the Enuma Elish. It relates how Marduk, the high god of Babylon, created the world. As with the Flood story, there are close parallels to and striking differences from the biblical account in Genesis 1. In both accounts, there is a common order to the creative process. Out of chaos emerges by divine initiative light, the firmament, the dry land, luminaries, and the human being. The apex of creation in the Enuma Elish, however, is the building of Babylon, where the gods rest. In Genesis 1:1–2:4a, it is the Sabbath *when* God rests, not a place but a time. The Enuma Elish is a political statement. There, Babylon is the first city created by the god who created the world.

As noted above, The New Jewish Version translates the first three verses of the Bible as follows:

> *When God began to create the heaven and the earth—the earth being unformed and void, with darkness over the surface of the deep and a wind from God sweeping over the water—God said, 'Let there be light'; and there was light.*

This translation is not based on any change in the Hebrew text; in fact, the traditional translation, "In the beginning. . .," had to alter the first word to achieve its rendering. The change, however, has profound theological implications. The traditional translation implies that God created matter out of nothing (the theory of *creatio ex nihilo*), which is not found in the Hebrew Bible but in the Apocrypha. The revised translation implies a pre-existent unformed matter. Creation here means formation. Light is created first, but it is not the light of the sun, which is created on the fourth day. In its usage throughout the Bible, God's light often means God's revelation. This is the case at the beginning of the Gospel of John, which is patterned after Genesis 1.

Genesis 1 may be seen as a reaction against the Enuma Elish. In terms of power and magnitude, nothing could exceed the claim of a god's authority to create the world. That claim did not originate with the Bible. But in its polytheistic context, it was so offensive to those who worshipped the God of Israel that it had to be rejected and the claim reserved for the one God who was not identified with the world in any respect. The pagan gods were a reflection of natural forces and human passions. Humans were their slaves and the establishment of Babylon as the first city gave the priests of Babylon an unexcelled region of authority. Genesis 1 is an apologetic statement. The God of Israel has no earthly location or physical identification. Only within the human being is the image of God found, but with no conceivable description.

It is notable that Jerusalem is not made the counterpart to Babylon. That elevated city with its glorified Temple, in which the Holy of Holies was seen as God's dwelling place for nearly 400 years, would seem to be uniquely qualified. But it was destroyed in 586 BCE. The language and style of Genesis 1 point to the Priestly tradition within the Jewish community of the Babylonian Exile. Here, the encounter with the Enuma Elish would have loomed large, demanding a response applicable to the Jews. Having lost their land, city, and temple, the reality of the living God was apparent even in a foreign land. No earthly form could claim his presence.

On the subject of creation, there is no necessary conflict between science and the Bible. That the order of creation in Genesis 1, going from the simple to the complex, the inanimate to the animate, the lower forms of life to the higher forms, is perceptive of some hierarchical structure is probably a refinement of phenomena long observed throughout the ancient Near East. However, the demythologization of the world in its early stages and reflected in this story allows for scientific investigation. One cannot, for example, analyze water as such which comes from a spring or river in which a god resides because god-water is not subject to examination.

The Garden of Eden Story

The Garden of Eden is surely one of the most notable passages in the Bible. Was it a place or a state of being? In some sense it was both. Regarding its place, there are a few helpful indicators. A river having four branches is said to flow out of the Garden (Genesis 2:10). The four names are given. Two of them represent the Tigris and Euphrates. The other two are not clearly identifiable but, as if the writer knew that they were not commonly known, the land areas where they flow are mentioned. One flows around Cush, the common name for Ethiopia. The other flows around Havilah, not a commonly known name but in the geographical genealogy of Genesis 10 a part of Cush.[3] Thus, perhaps, they are the Blue Nile and the White Nile. That makes the Garden of Eden the Fertile Crescent, the extended reaches of the known occupied world.

This identification is bolstered by references to Eden in the Book of Ezekiel. In his oracles against the nations, Ezekiel condemns the king of Tyre with all his opulence and finery, saying, "You were in Eden, the garden of God" (28:13). The pride of his heart corrupted him. Likewise, Pharaoh in his greatness is said to have been the tallest tree and "the envy of all the trees of Eden that were in the garden of God" (31:9). Like Tyre, Egypt was cast out of the garden.

The word Eden means luxury and delight. In the Genesis story, it is a state of being. In fact, the geographical references argue against its being a specific place but, rather, a symbol of the world. Adam is the Hebrew word for humankind, not a particular man. Eve is a transliteration of the Hebrew word for life. While the story is highly personalized, befitting the Hebraic literary genius, it defines the human condition and the human-divine relationship. The story of Adam and Eve is our story, the human story. That is surely its intent.

The Tower of Babel Story

The fourth of these major narratives which portray beginnings illustrates the human grasp for power. The Tower of Babel is a reflection of the temple towers of Mesopotamia, possibly the great Marduk temple, Etemenanki. The ancients thought that the high gods resided in the upper atmosphere, so temples were built on the tops of mountains. Lower Mesopotamia has no mountains; to compensate, temple towers were built. One may remember Jacob's dream in which a ladder or stairway reached from earth to heaven on which the angels of God were ascending and descending (Genesis 28:12).

The Tower of Babel story probably has an etiological function— that is, it serves to explain the multiplicity of languages. However, in assuming an original common language, it recognizes the family of languages common to the Fertile Crescent. The languages of Canaan with Arabic and Phoenician are interrelated but also share roots with the languages of Mesopotamia. Civilization in Mesopotamia is older, witness the focus of the whole of the Primeval History. Literary and cultural remains also confirm this. In the biblical story, the transition takes place when Abram journeys from Ur to Canaan.

The major emphasis of the Tower of Babel story is divine judgment on pride and the grasp for power. The human propensity to make a name, either individually or collectively, is among the strongest pursuits of self-gratification. Besides its general admonition, the story is a condemnation of Babylon, the name of which in Hebrew is *babel,* "gate of God." The explanation of the word as "confusion" is based on the play on the Hebrew word *balel,* which means to confuse. It is ironic that our language has adopted "babble" to mean confusing or meaningless speech.

The Primeval History a Myth-History

Looking at these four narratives, we can say that they are all rooted in traditions of Mesopotamia with a variety of connections. The ancient myths, the functions of the natural world, and political and cultural realities are represented. In all of them, however, the pervasive majesty of God is hovering, as it were, over the world. All the pagan accouterments have been shorn from them. And human beings, who emerge as God's creation, are given moral responsibilities. God's image is implanted in them. They are charged with care of the Earth. Their transgressions of the divine injunctions in the Garden of Eden lead to consequences of alienation and separation from God, of anguish, misery, or death. The Flood is made to be the ultimate judgment and the Tower of Babel, in arrogating the Name, the cardinal sin. Altogether, they depict the character of God and the character of human beings.

The Primeval History is all about beginnings. While it is presented in the guise of history, it is not history in our sense of the term. It is a uniquely fashioned kind of myth-history. In the briefest expanse, it tells us how the world came into being, how peoples emerged, the motivations of human beings, and God's all-encompassing presence and power. The past is in the East but it is dim and obscure. For the most part, it can be identified only by long lists of names, figures to whom are assigned exorbitant life spans. Only a few episodes are recounted, and these are mythic in character, apparently intended to tell not so much about the past as about reality in its universal sense. With all its brevity, it sets the stage for the story that is to be told, a story that is particular but has universal implications. This beginning enters the next stage by a geographical transition, the journey from Mesopotamia to Canaan. Indeed, at several crucial points, new stages in the story commence with a geographical transition.

The Story-History of the Patriarchs

The Primeval History represents a mythic past. The prologue, the patriarchal narratives, while not mythic, is not history either, although it establishes a setting for the major theme of the Old Testament, which is the formation, development, and character of the community of Israel. It gives an appearance of a pseudo-history.

The call of Abram-Abraham represents a watershed in this development. When the Lord, Yahweh, tells him to leave his country and his father's house, it means leaving the entire high civilization of Mesopotamia behind, including its complex polytheistic nature religion.

Abraham begins with a clean slate. He is not to look back but forward. His descendants will become a great nation and will possess the land of Canaan. Beyond this, what constitutes his blessing will be the means by which all other peoples are to find blessing. The rest of the Old Testament, of the Bible, of Jewish and Christian history, represent the attempt to realize the fulfillment of this magnanimous offer.

The patriarchs play a dual role in Genesis. They are presented as individuals in a family line culminating in the 12 sons of Jacob who, in Exodus, become the 12 tribes of Israel. They have direct, revelatory experiences of Yahweh, who mediates to them the blessing and the promise. At the same time, they are actors on the stage of the drama about God and Israel, providing the basics of the plot. They build altars to the Lord, as if founding some of the major cultic shrines operative throughout the peoples' history: Shechem, Bethel, Hebron, Salem (Jerusalem), and Beer-sheba. They deal with, but will not intermarry with, the peoples of the land. They banish foreign deities. They inaugurate the cultic practices of circumcision (17:9–14) and tithe (14:20; 28:22). A transition takes place when the entire family of Jacob moves down into Egypt and remains for 400 years. The wisdom given Joseph by Yahweh saves not only them but all the Egyptians.

The Bright-Thompson Debate

Are the narratives about the patriarchs history? This question represents a major storm center of Old Testament scholarship. There was much heated discussion about it during the mid- to late 20th century. Two schools have contested the issue. One, whose main defenders are known as the Albright school, from their founder William F. Albright, have emphasized "the essential historicity" of the patriarchs. The other group, called minimalists by the opposition, whose major spokesmen are Thomas Thompson and John Van Seters, deny any historicity.

John Bright of the Albright school states the problem clearly.

> *It is, let it be admitted, impossible in the proper sense to write a history of Israel's origins, and that because of limitations in the evidence both from archaeology and from the Bible itself. Even if we accept the Biblical account at face value, it is impossible to reconstruct the history of*

Israel's beginnings. Far too much is unknown. The Genesis narrative is painted in blacks and whites on a simple canvas with no perspective in depth. It depicts certain individuals and their families who move through their world almost as if they were alone in it. The great empires of the day, even the little peoples of Canaan, if they are introduced at all, are scarcely more than voices offstage. If Pharaohs of Egypt are allowed a modest part, they are not identified by name: We do not know who they were. In all the Genesis narrative no single historical figure is named who can, as yet, be otherwise identified. Nor has mention of any Hebrew ancestor demonstrably turned up in any contemporary inscription; since they were nomads of little importance, it is unlikely that any ever will. As a result, it is impossible to say within centuries when Abraham, Isaac, and Jacob actually lived. This alone would suffice to prevent the satisfactory writing of history.

Nor are we to overbid archaeological evidence. It cannot be stressed too strongly that in spite of all the light that it has cast on the patriarchal age, in spite of all that it has done to vindicate the antiquity and authenticity of the tradition, archaeology has not proved that the stories of the patriarchs happened just as the Bible tells them. In the nature of the case it cannot do so. At the same time—and this must be said with equal emphasis—no evidence has come to light contradicting the tradition. The witness of archaeology is indirect. It has lent to the picture of Israel's origins as drawn in Genesis a flavor of probability, and has provided the background for understanding it, but it has not proved the stories true in detail, and cannot do so. We know nothing of the lives of Abraham, Isaac, and Jacob save what the Bible tells us, the details of which lie beyond the control of archaeological data.[4]

Having said this, Bright examines the patriarchal narratives against the background of the early 2nd millennium in upper Mesopotamia from known written sources. The names Abram and Jacob appear in these sources. The customs of marriage, adoption, and inheritance are similar to those found in the Nuzi texts of the 15th century, but they are assumed to have existed in the earlier period also. The patriarchs are portrayed as pastoral nomads similar to those found in the Mari texts of the early 2nd millennium. There are other parallels.

> *The evidence so far adduced gives us every right to affirm that the patriarchal narratives are firmly based on history. . . . Although we cannot undertake to reconstruct the lives of Abraham, Isaac, and Jacob, we may confidently believe that they were actual historical individuals.*[5]

Thomas Thompson gave a thorough examination to the arguments advanced by Bright and found them all wanting. The name Abram is common to West Semitic culture but it, as well as the other patriarchal names, cannot be dated to any specific period.[6] And while the social customs "fit very well into the general context of ancient Near Eastern family law," they differ in many respects from the practices known from the Nuzi texts and from other extra-biblical sources.[7] Thompson's criticism, which applies to virtually all of the arguments of Bright and Albright regarding the historicity of the patriarchs, hinges on what constitutes evidence. He denies that they have provided any evidence for placing the patriarchs in the 2nd millenium BCE. Rather,

> *We can now say with some confidence that only during the Iron Age are all the cities of Palestine that are mentioned in the patriarchal narratives and which can be located with some certainty known and occupied.*[8]

Clues Related to Historicity

Several scholars have pointed out that the religion of the patriarchs was not institutional like later Israelite religion. There were no priests. They built altars but sacrifice is not associated with them; they were living memorials that became established shrines. The names for God are related to theophanies. They are El names, such as El-Bethel (35:7), God of Bethel; El-Elyon (14:22), God Most High; and El-Olam (21:23), Everlasting God. They antedate Yahwism. There is no awareness of the Canaanite religion which plagued the people of Israel throughout most of their history. This is consistent with the portrayal of the patriarchs as pastoral and not agricultural. Indeed, there is little awareness of other peoples in the land of Canaan except the Philistines, and they are known to appear there at the earliest in the 13th century BCE. Abram is said to have come from Ur of the Chaldeans (Genesis 11:28, 31). The Chaldeans are first mentioned in extra-biblical sources in the 11th century BCE.[9]

There are also some literary clues which have some bearing on the question of historicity. One finds a common story with some differences in details in three narratives, two associated with Abram (Genesis 12:10–20; 20) and one with Isaac (26:1–11). They are so similar that they point to a common origin suggesting that the details of at least two of them are not to be read as historical facts. In two different narratives (32:28 and 35:10), Jacob's name is changed, and in two different narratives, the city of Bethel is named (28:19 and 35:15). Rachel is said to have been buried near Bethlehem (35:19), whereas the tomb of Rachel is located in the territory of Benjamin in I Samuel 10:2. These and some other inconsistencies in the text detract from considering the narratives as history.

In the extensive genealogy of the Edomites, the statement is made: "These are the kings who reigned in the land of Edom before any king reigned over the Israelites" (36:31). This section could not have been written until the time of the Israelite kingdom, presumably long after the period of which it speaks. A similar gap in time is seen in the statements early in the Abraham narratives: "At that time the Canaanites were in the land" (12:6), and "At that time the Canaanites and the Perizzites lived in the land" (13:7). These statements assume that at the time of the writing, the Canaanites and Perizzites no longer lived in the land, suggesting a Judean perspective after the time of David because the Canaanites were never vanquished from the northern tribes or in the northern kingdom. One finds, also, an anachronistic statement in Genesis 14:14 where Abram is said to have gone "as far as Dan." According to Judges 18:29, the city of Dan was founded in the time of the judges, long after the time of the patriarchs, whenever that may have been.

Considering all of the factors mentioned above, we are left with patriarchal narratives which reflect geography and history of both the early and late 2nd millennium and of the Israelite kingdom. We must allow for the possibility that the tradition was modified as it was handed down.

While the patriarchs are commonly referred to as Abraham, Isaac, and Jacob, Isaac is little more than a transition figure. Like Abraham, he is primarily associated with the southern area and with the Philistines. Isaac and Jacob take wives who are Arameans, from the extended family of Abraham. These were from the region of Haran in upper Mesopotamia. Deuteronomy preserves an ancient confession which harks back to the early period: "A wandering Aramean was my father, he went down into Egypt and lived there as an alien . . ." (26:5). One suspects that the contention between Isaac and the Philistines over the digging of wells points to some historical situation, but there is no way to confirm it (Genesis 26).

The Jacob Story

The narratives about Jacob, which in a general way constitute the remainder of the Book of Genesis (27–50), divide into three groups: Jacob and Laban, Jacob and Esau, and Jacob and his sons. While all of these narratives are graphically personal, a great deal in them reflects the relationships between the peoples which the main characters represent. Several times, Laban is identified as an Aramean (25:20; 28:5; 31:20, 24), and the impact of these narratives is in showing how Jacob (Israel) becomes independent from Laban (Arameans) at Laban's (Aramean's) expense. The competition and conflict between Jacob and Laban may point to that of the northern kingdom of Israel (Jacob) with Syria (Aram) as we find it in the Books of Kings. While numerous references identify the ancestors of the Hebrew tribes as Arameans, the Jacob-Laban narratives serve to break the continuity and show the beginnings of a new people. Jacob's name is changed to Israel and his sons become the founders of the tribes.

The Jacob-Esau narratives, in similar fashion, represent the fratricidal struggle between Israel and the Edomites. In the story of their birth, Esau is said to be red and hairy, words in Hebrew remarkably close to Edom and Seir, Seir being the geographical region of the Edomites. Esau is characterized as rustic and easily duped; Jacob is quick-witted and tricky. In narratives of the wilderness wandering, Edom is recognized as a kingdom (in Numbers 20:14 as well as in Genesis 36) well before the time of the Israelite monarchy, but archaeological evidence dates it in Iron Age II (after 900 BCE). The early amicable relationship between the two peoples is seen in what is undoubtedly an old law in Deuteronomy 23:7: "You shall not abhor any of the Edomites, for they are your kin."

The severe enmity that developed between the two peoples began with David's wanton subjugation of Edom (II Samuel 8:13–14) and their revolt under Solomon (I Kings 11:14–22), achieving complete independence from Judah under Joram (II Kings 8:20–22). Isaac's limited blessing of Esau reads: ". . . you shall serve your brother; but when you break loose, you shall break his yoke from your neck" (Genesis 27:40). Revenge apparently came with the destruction of Jerusalem in 586 BCE. One of the exiles railed against the attackers, saying: "Remember, O Lord, against the Edomites the day of Jerusalem's fall, how they said, 'Tear it down! Tear it down! Down to its foundations'" (Psalms 137:7). In Malachi, from the same period, the Lord calls Edom, "the people with whom the Lord is angry forever" (1:4).

Some of the stories of Jacob and his sons reflect tribal character as depicted in later narratives while some of them seem unrelated to later tribal development. All of the sons except Benjamin are born in the region of Haran in upper Mesopotamia. Although Reuben is the first born, there is no recognition of his having first-born status. In these stories "the action is restricted almost entirely to the central hill country."[10] Rachel, the wife whom Jacob loves, bears two sons, Joseph and Benjamin, and their tribal counterparts were geographically located in the hill country. Benjamin, whose name means "son of the right hand" or "son of the south", occupied the small southern area, perhaps the size being associated with his being the youngest. The much larger northern hill country was settled by the tribes of Ephraim and Manasseh, Joseph's sons in these stories, while occasionally being referred to as Joseph.

Jacob is said to be the founder of Bethel, where the Lord extends to him the promise given to Abraham (28:18–22) and where his name is changed to Israel (35:10). He also buys property at Shechem (33:19). He erects altars in both places. These were among the most important tribal centers in the northern hill country. Shechem had long been an important Canaanite center. The story of Jacob's sons, Simeon and Levi, killing all the males and plundering the city because of Hamor's rape of Dinah (34) is undoubtedly a legend, given Shechem's size and importance known from archaeology and extra-biblical sources. Of course, it could be a contracted miniature of the takeover of the city by the Israelites. These two brothers are characterized in Jacob's last words (49:5–7) as fierce and cruel. It is notable that there is not even a hint of Levi's priestly role, which is so emphasized in later tradition, while the tribe of Simeon later lost recognition by being absorbed by Judah.

The tribe of Judah later became a territorial kingdom and

eventually survived all of the other tribes. In the patriarchal narratives, there is one long story about Judah. In relation to later tradition, which elevated Judah to the position of eminence in the political arena, it is not flattering. Judah marries a Canaanite woman and has sons by her. He is also tricked by his Canaanite daughter-in-law posing as a prostitute, whose services he utilizes and who conceives and bears him twins. One of these was named Perez and became the ancestor of David.

We must assume that this is an old story because later tradition condemned such intermarriage. Indeed, Abraham and Isaac deliberately avoided allowing their sons to marry any of the residents, suggesting either a different tradition or later influence upon the telling of these old stories. We must allow the possibility that narratives were modified by ongoing tradition as happens often with current religious traditions. The end of the Judah story in Genesis 38 provides the linkage between David and Judah. It is possible that this genealogy was appended to an already existing story.

The Joseph Novella

While the Joseph narratives are a novella about Joseph in particular, they belong in the larger sense to the story of Jacob and his sons. It has long been suggested that the Joseph story was written in the time of Solomon to provide a model for government officials. One section (Genesis 39–41), where there is no reference to Jacob or his other sons, emphasizes Joseph's character, acumen, and devotion to God despite unjust treatment.[11] His wisdom in understanding dreams and the ways of God elevate him to a position of supreme power in Egypt. His master's wife's attempt to seduce him bears a close parallel to that of an Egyptian story known as The Tale of Two Brothers. It is possible that this section was the original Joseph story around which the dramatic novella of Joseph and his brothers was woven. As Coates mentions, we can neither affirm nor deny the historicity of the Joseph legend on the basis of what we have.[12]

The Joseph novella is the story of a broken family. It is filled with irony and intrigue, which is evermore painful for Jacob and the brothers—even for Joseph, for whom the tension he creates is too much to bear. Yet justice demands that the brothers pay the penalty for selling him off, as if gone forever, and deceiving their father into thinking he had met a cruel death. One could say, of course, that the brother's hatred of Joseph is justified given his imperious self-image related in his dreams. But he attains the position of power upon which they are wholly dependent, and the resolution is a welcome relief to all of them.

Jacob, too, receives his just desserts. He had tricked his father, Isaac, into giving him the blessing which rightfully belonged to his brother, Esau, and now he in turn is tricked by his sons into believing that Joseph is dead, grieving for years before learning that Joseph is alive, after which he spends his final years in Joseph's care.

Politically, the Joseph novella elevates the tribes of the northern hill country: Ephraim, Manasseh, and Benjamin. Joseph, of course, towers over all the others. But it is Ephraim and Manasseh who receive the deathbed blessing of Jacob. Benjamin is recognized as the most precious of the sons of Jacob; when the brothers go to Egypt, Joseph sets him apart with more ample provisions. Moreover, Joseph's cup is deliberately placed in Benjamin's sack.

A Tribal Story-History Poem

The so-called Blessing of Jacob (Genesis 49) is part blessing and part curse in characterizing the political fortunes or misfortunes of the 12 tribes. Reuben, the first born, while not cursed is condemned for violating his father's bed, an incident noted in 35:22. In terms of tribal history, we have no indication of it. Simeon and Levi are cursed because of their violence toward men and beasts, for which they are to be scattered in Israel. Simeon, amalgamated with Judah, finally loses its identity. Levi also ceases from having tribal status but either by transformation or new birth becomes a guild of priests. Genesis knows nothing of this later function.

Judah and Joseph are given the most generous blessings by far. Judah holds the scepter, a symbol of authority, "until Shiloh comes" or "until he comes to Shiloh" (the literal translation of 49:10). The temple at Shiloh was the central shrine before that of Jerusalem (I Samuel 1–4; Jeremiah 7:12). While Judah under David and Solomon ruled the tribal confederation, it was a prophet from Shiloh, Ahijah, who initiated the rebellion of the northern tribes, ending the United Monarchy (I Kings 11:29–39).[13]

The blessing of Joseph is rich and passionately full. Progeny and fruitfulness of the land are to be his, endlessly supported by the Mighty One of Jacob, known also by many other names, including Protector. Joseph is set apart from his brothers. He had been given the region of Shechem by Jacob, who had bestowed blessings on Ephraim and Manasseh, Joseph's sons (48:8–22). Joseph is later buried at Shechem (Joshua 24:32).

The remaining tribes receive brief descriptive treatment. It is fitting that this old poem be placed near the end of Genesis because it provides the transition from stories about Jacob's sons as individuals to their representation as tribes, as the introduction and conclusion of the poem indicate. But the end of the book (50:15–21) portrays the sons as individuals again, undoubtedly to serve a theological purpose. Joseph's brothers are fearful that he will take revenge on them for having sold him off. He, on the other hand, attributes this to the fulfillment of God's purpose, that the whole of his father's family should be preserved.

Conclusion

Genesis is a collection of stories placed in a pseudo-historical framework, starting from the beginning of time and moving to the point where Israel has become a people. These stories bear some distant relation, geographically and politically, to Mesopotamia, the land of Canaan and Egypt. While there are extra-biblical parallels to stories in the Primeval History, as already noted, and to an incident in the Joseph stories, noted above, the patriarchal characters are unknown outside the biblical narratives.

The overarching theme of the book of Genesis is the activity of God. God stands above and behind the world as a whole but is active in initiating the formation of a people who are to be set apart from all other peoples. Abraham is the father of this people. The other patriarchs in turn are agents of the divine purpose as the promise of the eventual people of God is given. God calls and guides Abraham, wrestles with Jacob and overwhelms him in a dream, and is ever present in the background of Joseph's life journey.

The pseudo-history of Genesis is the story of God revealing himself in the world of time, which is the world of human beings. Sometimes these humans are generic, representing what humans are like; sometimes they are individuals illustrating emotions and actions in given circumstances; sometimes they are representative of peoples: tribes within Israel, those closely associated within the region of Canaan, and peoples known by tradition and lore. But the human development is invariably linked to the divine process. Each episode plays a part, whether small or large, whether remote or central, whether moral or cultic, in telling the story of God. 📖

Notes

1.E. A. Speiser, *Genesis* (New York: Doubleday, 1964), 35–43.

2. John Bright, "Has Archaeology Found Evidence of the Flood" in *The Biblical Archaeologist Reader,* ed. Wright and Freedman (Garden City:Doubleday, 1961), 32–40.

3. Yohanan Aharoni and Michael Avi-Yonah, *The Macmillan Bible Atlas* (New York: Macmillan, 1993), 21.

4. John Bright, *A History of Israel,* 3rd ed. (Philadelphia: Westminster Press, 1981), 74–75.

5. Ibid., 92.

6. Thomas Thompson, *The Historicity of the Patriarchal Narratives* (Berlin: Walter de Gruyter, 1974), 36.

7. Ibid., 294–295.

8. Ibid., 325.

9. H. Jagersma, *A History of Israel in the Old Testament Period,* trans. John Bowden (Philadelphia: Fortress Press, 1983), 14.

10. Yohanan Aharoni and Michael Avi-Yonah, 44.

11. For more, see George W. Coates, "Joseph, Son of Jacob" in *Anchor Bible Dictionary,* 3:980.

12. Ibid., 980.

13. See Bruce Dahlberg, "Genesis" in *Mercer Commentary on the Bible* (Macon: Mercer University Press, 1995), 124.

Exodus, Leviticus, Numbers

Israel's Spiritual Formation

The word pentateuch is a Greek word meaning "five books." It probably originated in the Greek-speaking Jewish community as the designation of "The Five Books of Moses." This is the Hebrew "Torah" or "The Law of Moses." Strictly speaking, however, there are only four books of Moses. The birth of Moses occurs at the beginning of Exodus; his death comes at the conclusion of Deuteronomy; and he dominates the four books with an overwhelming presence. The book of Jubilees, one of the Pseudepigrapha, explains that an angel revealed the whole of Genesis and the first 19 chapters of Exodus—Moses' own life experience—to Moses on Mt. Sinai.[1] Thus, tradition refers to "The Five Books of Moses."

Four Equals Three Plus One

There is a sense of unity about these four books. That unity is expressed in the constant awareness of the intimate relationships between God, Moses, and Israel. The bulk of this material is law; indeed, all of the law in the Old Testament, strictly speaking, is contained in these four books. In its current and final setting, all of it is said to be divinely mediated through Moses in the wilderness. In reality, it represents the accumulation of laws within the communities of Israel during the entire period of Israel's existence in the land of Canaan, from its emergence there in the 13th century BCE through the time of the Babylonian Exile in the late 6th century BCE or later. Law emerges as the need for it emerges, reflecting the social, political, and religious values amid the sometimes changing circumstances of life. Consequently, there are several different groupings of law coming from different periods and different geographical settings.

While these four books in the present arrangement are bound together by the figure of Moses and the law which he mediates, on closer examination the Book of Deuteronomy should be seen as a separate entity on both literary and theological grounds. It seems to have been edited and reworked to accommodate to the Kingdom of Judah in the late 8th and 7th centuries BCE, although the bulk of it belongs to the northern Kingdom of Israel before its fall in 722 BCE. It was not uncommon for the ancient traditions to be modified and added to where they had an ongoing application to the society's well-being. This poses difficulties for us in determining the earlier from the later but, of course, the material must have been highly important to warrant continued appeal and usage.

The books of Exodus, Leviticus, and Numbers are linked together by one major literary-theological unit that may be called the Sinai Event or the Tabernacle Theology. A secondary theme, the Wilderness Journey, begins in Exodus and continues to the end of Numbers. A third theme, Deliverance from Egyptian Bondage, opens the Book of Exodus. Both of the two groupings—Exodus-Leviticus-Numbers and Deuteronomy—exercise theological influence on the Book of Joshua. Deuteronomy becomes the controlling influence on Judges, Samuel, and Kings. Exodus-Leviticus-Numbers becomes closely related to Ezra-Nehemiah and Chronicles; indeed, Ezra-Nehemiah provides the post-exilic historical setting for the cultic oriented story histories of Exodus-Leviticus-Numbers and Chronicles. It may be a useful oversimplification to suggest that these two traditions may be labeled prophetic and priestly. The prophetic emphasis on obedience to the righteous will of Yahweh dominates the legal and history-story material in Deuteronomy, Judges, Samuel, and Kings, whereas the description of the cult and the appeal to cultic faithfulness characterize the traditions in Exodus-Leviticus-Numbers and Ezra-Nehemiah.

Moses

Moses is an elusive figure. At times, he appears as a very human being as, for example, when he marries a Cushite woman, antagonizing Miriam and Aaron (Numbers 12:1) or when he confesses his inadequacy to accept the Lord's call to leadership (Exodus 3:7–4:17). At other times, he takes on superhuman characteristics. In the battle against the Amalekites, Israel prevails as long as Moses holds up his hands or as long as his hands are held up by someone else (Exodus 17:8–13). When Moses comes down from the mountain after speaking with God, his face shines so that he has to cover it with a veil except when he speaks with God (Exodus 34:29–35).

The historicity of Moses is fraught with numerous questions. As already noted, Moses is the agent who communicates to Israel all the collections of laws even though some of them reflect the early tribal period and some the post-exilic priestly community, a separation of several centuries. The birth of Moses has legendary characteristics. He is presented as the first born of Levite parents, although he has a brother who is three years older as well as a grown sister (Exodus 2:1–4; 7:7). The story of being placed in a basket on the river and being found by Pharaoh's daughter is paralleled by that of the Babylonian king, Sargon.[2]

There is one clue that suggests when Moses actually lived. It is found in Judges 18:30, a text that was tampered with by the scribes to try to protect Moses from the taint of his grandson's idolatry. They half-changed the name "Moses" to "Manasseh" by inserting a suspended "n", although Gershom is mentioned as his son, as in other places. This gives the original text a ring of authenticity. If Moses' grandson was a priest at Dan in the early part of the 12th century BCE[3], that would place Moses in the middle of the 13th century BCE or thereabouts, the time traditionally associated with the wilderness wanderings.

The Deliverance from Egypt

The story of the deliverance from Egypt is high drama. Literarily, it is told in the form of a contest, a contest between the supreme political power in the southern Fertile Crescent in the Late Bronze Age and a group of slaves within its borders yearning to be free. These slaves were Hebrews who were bound together by worshipping a single god, Yahweh. While the setting is within Egypt proper, it should be noted that during this period Egypt controlled the land of Canaan by established government of a number of city-states there. The Amarna letters (14th century BCE), written by the governing officials in Canaan to the home base in Egypt, complain about rebellious people known as Apiru or Habiru, names that may be related to Hebrew. Whether or not the Exodus story reflects events in the land of Canaan as well as in Egypt proper is hard to say. The contest has a legendary character. We do not know what kind of history lies behind it.

The contest between Yahweh and Pharaoh is a cosmic event. Like that other great contest in the Old Testament—the one on Mt. Carmel between Yahweh and Baal (I Kings 18)—it is a question of who is in control, who holds the real power. Was it the god of the greatest earthly kingdom, with its high culture—for Pharaoh was not only a king but was revered as a god—or was it the god WHO IS (Exodus 3:14) and who brings freedom to the powerless? Moses and Aaron were Yahweh's agents even as Elijah was Yahweh's agent on Mt. Carmel.

The contest begins with a trick that challenges the magicians of Egypt. Aaron turns his staff into a snake. The magicians do the same. Then come the plagues. The first plague (Exodus 7:17–24)is onerous and pervasive. Moses strikes the Nile with his staff and all the water in Egypt is turned to blood. Ironically, the magicians do the same. The irony is not only in there being no water left to repeat the trick but in acting against their own people. The second plague (Exodus 8:1–7), the invasion of frogs, puts the magicians in the same position. Frogs are said to be everywhere after Aaron stretched forth his hand over the waters, even in the ovens and kneading bowls. Of course, one does not ask if Aaron traveled to all the pools, canals, and rivers in Egypt to stretch forth his hand. This is the stuff of story. And, again, the magicians perform the same trick.

The third plague (Exodus 8:16–19), a horde of gnats, stretches the magicians' skills beyond their abilities. In bowing out of the contest, they recognize in their defeat the "finger of God," but Pharaoh is relentless in not giving in. The fourth plague (Exodus 8:20–24) brings swarms of flies, and now the Lord insulates the land of Goshen, where the Hebrews live, from this and further plagues, although nothing was said previously about their being affected by the first three plagues. With the fourth plague, also, Pharaoh begins to accede to Moses' request to let the Hebrews leave to worship the Lord. He will allow them to sacrifice but only within the land. He also asks Moses to pray for him. The tide is beginning to turn even though Pharaoh hardens his heart and will not let the people go following each plague.

The fifth plague (Exodus 9:1–7) kills all of the domestic animals of the Egyptians, but the sixth plague (Exodus 9:8–12), the infestation of boils, is said to have infected humans *and* animals. Apparently, the writer forgot that all of the animals had been killed off in the previous plague. The animals are also affected by the seventh plague (Exodus 9:22–26), destructive hail. Not only animals and humans that were out in the open but all plants and trees are killed off. Pharaoh now confesses that he has sinned, that the Lord is right, and that he will let the Hebrews go. But when the hail stops, he reneges.

With the threat of invading locusts, Pharaoh agrees to allow the men to leave but not the children. This is, of course, unacceptable, so the Lord tells Moses to stretch out his staff over the land to bring the locusts, the eighth plague (Exodus 10:12–20). When they come, they devour everything that the hail left. Pharaoh confesses his sin again and asks Moses to pray for him, which he does. The locusts are driven back and the Lord hardens Pharaoh's heart. This poses an antinomy. The Lord is punishing Pharaoh and his people for refusing to allow the Hebrews to leave but at the same time is controlling Pharaoh's will in refusing the request. In this story, the Lord is in control of all the factors, a theological emphasis given in addition to the ethical point that the powerful are oppressors of the powerless.

The ninth plague (Exodus 10:21–28) is complete darkness in all Egypt except where the Israelites live. Pharaoh now yields somewhat more. He will allow all the Hebrews to go but they may not take their animals. Moses explains that animals are necessary for sacrifice. Again the Lord hardens Pharaoh's heart and this time he expels Moses unconditionally. There will be no further negotiations.

The 10th and final plague (Exodus 11:4–8; 12:29–32) brings the contest to a climax. It is the death of the firstborn. The first eight plagues are natural phenomena that some have tried to explain as being causatively connected. The flooded Nile is said to have a blood-red color. It deposits dead fish and the water is undrinkable. Frogs sometimes emerge which invade the land. Insects multiply from the rotting fish and frogs. Boils come from the infecting insects. And so on. While these phenomena may serve as material for the legend, they can hardly support any historical claim because of their recurring nature. Pharaoh is unnamed and could be any Pharaoh or all Pharaohs.

That the death of the firstborn is the decisive factor in the contest, irreversibly changing Pharaoh's mind, so that he not only urges Moses and Aaron to lead the Israelites out of Egypt to worship the Lord but also asks that he be blessed, shows how powerful this symbol is in the tradition. Further, it is presented as an envelope figure, encasing the long statement of regulations about the celebration of the Passover. The plague is announced, the particulars for eating the Passover and Unleavened Bread are given, and all the firstborn of the Egyptians are slain. But it is also an envelope figure for the entire story of the plagues. After Moses is called to go down into Egypt, the Lord says that he will harden Pharaoh's heart.

> Then you shall say to Pharaoh, "Thus says the Lord: Israel
> is my firstborn son. I said to you, 'Let my son go that he may
> worship me.' But you refused to let him go: now I will kill
> your firstborn son." (Exodus 4:22–23)

What is the import of this symbol that poses the consummate contrast between the highly cultured and powerful Egypt and the undistinguished and powerless Israel? It means that Israel is the firstborn among the nations, and accorded a different kind of status as a people, because it has been chosen by God.

The 10th plague serves a secondary purpose. It provides the backdrop for one of the most important festivals in Israelite history: Passover (Exodus 12:1–27). Thought to be originally two independent festivals observed in agricultural societies—the other, Unleavened Bread—and later combined into one, the Israelites transformed these as well as other nature festivals into historic remembrances. Thus, Passover became the means of remembering the deliverance from Egypt even as the Feast of Booths, an autumn agricultural festival, serves to remember the wilderness journey. It is at the point of greatest tension in the story of the plagues, when the movement has reached its climax in the 10th plague, that the ordinance of Passover abruptly interrupts the process. The death of all the firstborn has just been announced by Moses to Pharaoh. This ordinance reads as a practice for all time with explicit instructions. Here it is oblivious of the heightened contest. It assumes a settled society applicable to everyone "whether an alien or a native of the land" (12:19).

After the completion of the ordinance, the narrative returns to the action of the 10th plague. The firstborn of the Egyptians are slain and the Israelites take off in a hurry with the unleavened bread in their bowls (12:29–36). The contest is finished, or almost. The final scene of this great drama is yet to come.

Obviously, the Deliverance from Egypt as recorded in the Book of Exodus is not an historical event. It appears, rather, to be a mythic representation of, perhaps, a long and drawn-out struggle of a sub-servient people in gaining their freedom from a ruling empire through the power of a living God who claimed them for his own. The story of the plagues is fittingly introduced by Moses' encounter with Yahweh in the environs of Mt. Horeb (Exodus 3ff.), the name of the sacred mountain more common to Deuteronomy. Mostly in Exodus-Leviticus-Numbers, the name Sinai is found. The burning bush is symbolic, for fire is a common feature of Yahweh theophanies. That the bush is not consumed means that the fire burns continuously, that Yahweh is an unending active Presence. His name means "to be," "to be present," or "to cause to be" (3:14). There has been much discus-sion about this. In spite of Moses' self-deprecation, Yahweh will give him the power to work wonders. A reluctant Moses becomes the medi-ator in the process of liberating the Israelites from the Egyptians.

This preface (Exodus 1:1–7:7) to the story of the plagues is also a preface to the more far-reaching purpose of overcoming all the obsta-cles in pursuit of the possession of the land of Canaan, a theme which stretches not only to the end of the Book of Numbers but ultimately to the end of the Book of Joshua. The voice heard from the burning bush echoes this primary emphasis of the gift of the land of Canaan (3:8). That larger purpose is first stated at the beginning of the patriarchal nar-ratives (Genesis 12:1) and is restated, not only in this theophany where Yahweh first reveals his name to Moses, but on the second occasion when he reveals his identity with God Almighty (El Shaddai), the God of the Patriarchs (Exodus 6:4,8). Amid its numerous stories, small and large, the theme of the settlement of the land of Canaan through the Lord's guidance and power is the most comprehensive, binding together the first six books of the Old Testament into what is known as the Hexateuch.

The Journey Tradition

The Journey Tradition now begins at Exodus 12:37: "The Israelites journeyed from Rameses to Succoth . . ." Then, rather abruptly, at verse 43, an additional regulation on Passover is given. No foreigner or uncircumcised man may eat it but a slave who has been circumcised may eat it. Obviously, this reflects a period when Israel was settled in the land. The recently freed slaves could hardly own slaves themselves. The regulation is obviously an afterthought, perhaps a later addition recognizing circumstances unforeseen earlier. But the insertion of cultic ordinances is found here and there in this journey tradition. The pattern continues in chapter 13 with the stipulation to consecrate the firstborn (verses 1–2). Immediately, the subject changes to the celebration of the Feast of Unleavened Bread as a remembrance of the deliverance from Egypt (verses 3–10), strengthening the assumption that Passover and Unleavened Bread were originally independent festivals. Following this, the description of the dedication of the firstborn returns and is given full expression (verses 11–16).

The most striking and well-known feature of the Deliverance from Egypt story is the parting of the Red Sea. The Lord drives back the sea with a great wind and the Israelites walk across on dry land with the angel of God behind them. When the Egyptians pursue and their chariots become clogged, the Lord tells Moses to stretch his hand over the sea and the water returns to its normal place, drowning the Egyptians. And Moses sings a song of praise (15:1–18) as do Miriam and all the women in dance (15:20–21).

The Journey Tradition continues, characterized by the complaining of the Israelites and the sustaining of them by the Lord through his provisions of food and water. These themes of the people wanting to go back to Egypt, of the provision of quails and manna, of Moses striking the rock for water, appear again in the Journey Tradition in Numbers. The organization of judges in Exodus 18, however, is unique. Under the influence of Jethro, his father-in-law, Moses appoints a hierarchy of judges. While this chapter is placed in the setting of the wilderness wanderings, it reflects a settled society, for Jethro ends his advice to Moses in saying, "All these people will go to their home in peace" (18:23).

History or Story

The narrative of the Exodus and the wilderness wandering is theological legend. Finkelstein and Silberman have gleaned the pertinent information about Egypt and Canaan from historical and archaeological sources.[4] From early times, there is abundant evidence of people from Canaan going to Egypt when drought or famine occurred. During the 17th and 16th centuries BCE, a Canaanite people, traditionally known as the Hyksos, effectively ruled Egypt. But they were driven out. In a late 13th-century BCE manuscript, the names of the cities Succoth and Pithom are mentioned in relation to peoples migrating into Egypt. The city of Rameses, named for the 13th-century Pharaoh, has been located in the delta. All three of these cities belong to the Exodus narrative. But there is found no reference to Israel in these sources.[5]

The name "Israel" does occur once, on a stele of the late 13th-century Pharaoh Merneptah, among the enemies he has defeated, saying: "Israel is laid waste, his seed is not."[6] This is the earliest extra-biblical reference to Israel and the only one from this early period. Merneptah, of course, may have been boasting. But it is an historical fact that a people known as "Israel" was in the land of Canaan in the 13th century BCE.

Archaeology has found nothing to support the narrative about the Exodus and the wilderness wandering. The site of Kadesh-Barnea, where the Israelites were settled during much of the story of the wandering (Numbers 13:26; 20:1), shows no evidence of occupation during the Late Bronze and Early Iron Ages (before 1000 BCE). The same can be said for Arad, and Heshbon yielded only sparse remains from Iron Age I.[7] Balaam is mentioned as a seer in plaster inscriptions of the 8th and 7th centuries, but in a tradition unrelated to Numbers 22–24.[8] Edom did not exist as a kingdom during this period.

However, as I discovered during a summer on an archaeological expedition, a strong local Moses tradition is associated with the city of Petra, biblical Sela (II Kings 14:7), through which passes Wadi Musa, the Valley of Moses. The Spring of Moses, which gushes continuously, is just outside the city. On the vertical face of one of the mountains, water seeps constantly, a reminder of the incident where Moses struck the rock for water (Numbers 20:2–13). The tallest mountain of Petra is Jebel Harun (Mt. Aaron), the biblical Mt. Hor, where Aaron is said to have died (Numbers 20:22–29). To be sure, one cannot date these traditions, but they cannot be ignored. Since several of them are associated

with a common location, we are inclined to believe that they are witness
to something historical about Moses and Aaron, but that that something
cannot be specified.

I must conclude that the present narrative is highly fictionalized.
The figure of 600,000 men in addition to women and children (Exodus
12:37; Numbers 1:46; 26:51) is many times what the wilderness could
sustain. Anyone familiar with the area knows that while the Bedouin
pasture small flocks of sheep and goats over wide-ranging terrain, large
animals cannot be supported by that barren area. The picture of the
organization of the tribes in Numbers 1:1–10:28 with three of them on
each side of the Tabernacle that is surrounded immediately by the
Levites, all marching in designated order, is surely a theological con-
struct. This is magnified by the identical offerings made by each tribe
for the dedication of the altar, including silver plates, choice flour with
oil, gold dishes, bulls, and oxen, all of which are so far removed from
what the desert supplies that factual attribution is beyond all question
(Numbers 7).

This story is of an idealized past as an example for a community
where temple worship is central, apparently post-exilic Judaism. The
wilderness functions here like an island, unrelated to the rest of the
world, where the Lord provides all that is needed and Israel is given the
structure for functioning as a holy people. The focus is on the center of
the sanctuary toward which all Israel brings its gifts and recognition of
failures, and from which holiness exudes to cleanse and nurture the
community.

The Sinai Event

I have noted that Moses dominates all four of these books but that
I must separate Deuteronomy from the first three simply because it tells
a different story, as will be noted in the following chapter. Exodus,
Leviticus, and Numbers are inextricably bound together by the Sinai
event which begins at Exodus 19 and goes through the remainder of
Exodus, the whole of Leviticus, and the first part of Numbers through
10:28. This section defines Israel's spiritual formation in terms of
priestly centered worship and conduct. The Lord speaks the keynote at
the outset: "You shall be to me a kingdom of priests and a holy nation"
(Exodus 19:6).

One of the difficulties in summarizing a large block of biblical material is that invariably a major coherent literary unit has accrued smaller units of tradition around it that may complicate understanding the larger unit. There seems to have been a desire to include revered traditions, sometimes similar in type and sometimes diverse, even at the expense of the larger unity.

The Sinai Event is a fitting example. The larger unit, which I have called the Tabernacle Theology, describes the ideal institution: the Tabernacle, with its furnishings attended by the first order of priests (Exodus 25–31, 35–40); the sacrifices, laws of clean and unclean, proper sexual and moral relationships, festivals, property, and care of the environment, vows (Leviticus); and the formation and positioning of the ideal Israel (Numbers 1:1–10:28). The editors of the Sinai Event provided a preface (Exodus 19) filled with terrifying volcanic psychological imagery, which seems to be intended to prepare the reader for the gravity of the words that are to be spoken. All Israel surrounds Mt. Sinai having washed their clothes and been consecrated by Moses. The mountain is electrically charged and wrapped in smoke. Moses goes up to receive the law.

In the midst of this *mysterium tremendum* comes Israel's most universal code of laws, the Ten Commandments (Exodus 20:1–17). That it held an independent status is seen by its other appearance in Deuteronomy 5:6–21. These commandments seem to have been originally very brief as a few of them remain. Some grew with tradition, especially the one on the Sabbath, by far the longest, where there are substantial differences between the two versions.

The Covenant Code

There follows what is, perhaps, the oldest biblical code of laws applicable to an agricultural community, the Covenant Code (21:1–23:19). In it, there are very few references which define this community. There is no mention of Israel or any of the tribes, but those addressed are to remember that they were aliens in Egypt. They are to attend festival three times a year before the Lord God, but no specific place is mentioned, only the house of the Lord, wherever that may be. There is no mention of priests, but there are judges. Lawsuit is recognized, but difficult cases are to be brought before God, without specifying the human agent or place.

Slaves were members of this community. They could be bought and sold, but only within the community. There were rules governing the conditions of their enslavement. Apparently, slavery was a means of social welfare, allowing people who were victims of dire circumstances to survive.

This code clearly applies to a specific settled community practicing agriculture. It calls for respect for a community leader, whoever he may be. It shows no relationship to other communities except to apply equal protection to resident aliens. What suggests the early period is that there is no entrenched organization exercising authority. There is some kind of religious center where three yearly festivals are observed and where the most difficult judicial cases are brought. But the focus of the code as a whole is on family and community functioning. Politically and geographically, it could have applied to one or several areas, but they all belonged to the group that had been in Egypt.

At the end of the Covenant Code, the Journey Tradition resumes (23:20), but only briefly: "I am going to send an angel in front of you, to guard you on the way and to bring you to the place that I have prepared." The inhabitants of the land of Canaan are to be driven out little by little.

Chapter 24 serves as a transition between the Covenant Code and the Tabernacle Theology. It is composed of brief narratives that alternate between those that elevate the priestly contingency to positions of nearness to the God of Israel on Mt. Sinai in preparation for Moses to receive the Tabernacle Theology at the apex (verses 1–2, 9–11, 15–18) and those that confirm the two codes already given, namely, the Covenant Code and the Ten Commandments (verses 3–8, 12–14). In the former, Aaron and his sons go partway up the mountain with Moses where they see God, elsewhere forbidden. Moses, alone, goes to the top. In the latter, Moses seals the covenant with sacrificial blood and, with Joshua, ascends the mountain to receive the tablets of stone. Aaron and Hur are left with the people. This narrative leads directly to 31:18 and chapters 32–34.

The Community of Holiness—
Separated From the World

At the heart of these three books—Exodus, Leviticus, and Numbers—is a full-blown picture of a community so highly structured and so worship oriented that it serves to define the devout life through cultic obedience. It begins at Exodus 24:15 and goes through the remainder of Exodus (except for the intrusive chapters 31:18–34:35), the whole of Leviticus, and Numbers to 10:28. It represents the community of Israel as it ought to be from the point of view of the priesthood. It is the hypothetical Tabernacle World. Yet within this idealistic construction, the positions and practices of the priesthood and the regulations applicable to the community seem to reflect some genuine historical reality, though not in the wilderness setting.

The wilderness is the ideal place for this picture because it excludes all outside influences. There are no alien peoples to lure or to challenge, no outside world with its cultures. Israel need only concentrate on the particulars related to living a pure and holy life.

Central to this picture is the presence of the Lord (Yahweh). The larger cultic epic, the Sinai Event, begins with Exodus 19, where Israel arrives in the wilderness of Sinai and encamps around the mountain. Yahweh's presence is above this mountain. The crucial events take place in the encounters between Yahweh and Moses. Yahweh descends to the top of the mountain in the midst of a thick cloud that covers everything, accompanied by thunder, lightning, and a long trumpet blast, causing the whole mountain to shake and be electrically charged. This is psychological imagery appropriate to the gravity of dispensing the Law. The whole Law in this epic is given to Moses on top of Mt. Sinai. There is one small problem here, not with the mediatorship of Moses but where the transmission takes place. The Book of Leviticus opens with the statement that the Lord spoke the laws that follow from the Tent of Meeting. However, three times at the end of the book (25:1, 26:46, 27:34) they are said to have been given to Moses on Mt. Sinai. Likely, the statement at the beginning of Leviticus was influenced by the ending of Exodus where Yahweh enters the Tabernacle.

The Tabernacle

The first order of priority in Israel's response to the giving of the Law is the construction of the Tabernacle. Yahweh must have a dwelling place. He says, "Have them make me a sanctuary, so that I may dwell among them" (25:8). This is a momentous event in Israel's mythic memory. Yahweh will make a transition from Mt. Sinai, a cosmic habitation with all its forces that can shake the universe, to a windowless room containing the ark holding "the testimony," a code of law that is not defined. To be sure, a cloud covers the Tabernacle during the day and gives the appearance of fire at night (Numbers 9:15), but Yahweh's presence is in the Tabernacle. The implication of this transition is from a God who is transcendent and distant to a God who is near and imminent. The law is all about living a life of holiness in community.

The symbolism reflected in the Tabernacle suggests that it is more of an ideal object than an historical structure.

> *First, the dimension of the tabernacle and all its parts reflect a carefully contrived design and a harmonious whole. The numbers 3, 4, 10 predominate with proportionate cubes and rectangles. The various parts—the separate dwelling place, the tent, and the court—are all in exact numerical relation. The use of metals—gold, silver, and copper—are carefully graded in terms of their proximity to the Holy of Holies. In the same way, the particular colors appear to bear some inner relation to their function, whether the white, blue, or crimson. There is likewise a gradation in the quality of the cloth used. Finally, much stress is placed on the proper position and orientation, with the easterly direction receiving the place of honor.[9]*

Likewise, were the Tabernacle to be considered an actual object, one would need to account for the skills required for its construction and the source of these costly materials, neither of which would have been the common property of a group of freed slaves wandering in the wilderness.

> *There were gifted foremen who are mentioned by name, and with them a list of helpers. But even so, were all the skills of joinery, embroidery, casting, etc., present to the degree required for the erection of the tabernacle? Several centuries later, Solomon for his temple had to have recourse to Phoenician skilled labor for his metal work (I Kings 5:6; 7:13–14,40,45). Then, too, the amounts of the materials required are very considerable. Precious stones, linen, dyes, oil for the lamps, not to mention about 1¼ tons of gold, about 4 tons of silver, and about 3 tons of bronze.[10]*

From the time of Julius Wellhausen, who finalized the

Documentary Hypothesis as the modern theory of the authorship of the Pentateuch in the late 19th century, the Tabernacle has been seen as reflecting the basic plan of Solomon's Temple.[11]

> *Above all, the Priestly account records a structure that, in its shape and the cultic objects it contains, resembles Solomon's Temple. What it presents is a description of the Temple under the guise of a portable sanctuary. It is thus a retrojection of the Jerusalem Temple to the wilderness epoch, in accordance with the Priestly view that all Israel's institutions originated at that time, but with the knowledge that a permanent building did not exist before the settlement in Canaan.[12]*

While the Tabernacle bears the theological pattern of the Temple, it assumes the form of a tent. There are numerous references to a tent in earlier traditions, including the Journey Tradition of the wilderness wandering found in Exodus 31:18–34:35, continuing the narrative from the end of chapter 24. Here, Moses pitched the tent, but he pitched it outside the camp (33:7–11), whereas the Tabernacle occupied the center of the camp (Numbers 2). This tent served a different function from the Tabernacle. It was where the Lord spoke directly with Moses, not an elaborate facility for priestly ministrations as was the Tabernacle.

There are a few other striking differences between these two traditions. In the priestly tradition, Aaron and his sons are the only designated priests in perpetuity. Their elegant adornment befits their paramount position in the functioning of the cult (Exodus 28). The Levites are the priests' assistants, charged with caring for the Tabernacle and its furnishings (Numbers 3). In the older tent tradition, Aaron, while a close associate of Moses, becomes an apostate in building a golden calf to be worshiped. The Levites ordain themselves by slaughtering the backsliders who followed Aaron (Exodus 32). In this tradition, also, Joshua is Moses' assistant who cares for the tent (Exodus 33:11). He is not present in the priestly tradition.

I have said that the books of Exodus, Leviticus, Numbers, and Deuteronomy are the four books of Moses and may be thought of under the designation Israel's Spiritual Formation. I have found that Exodus, Leviticus, and Numbers represent a literary unit because the center half, when grouped together (Exodus 25 through Numbers 10:28—except for

Exodus 31:18–34:35 which would better follow Exodus 24) is a unified and complete picture of the priestly pattern of worship. It is a harmonious whole. It is the Tabernacle Theology. Deuteronomy, it will be seen, stands on its own and is more closely related to the historical books that follow: Joshua (which also reflects priestly tradition), Judges, Samuel, and Kings.

The magnitude of the Tabernacle as the divine abode is seen not only in the exquisite materials and workmanship but in the fact that the scenario of its formation is given twice: first in the plan of the Tabernacle with the ark, the table, the lamp stand, and the altars, along with the plan for the consecration of Aaron and his sons (Exodus 25:1–31:17); then all the particulars are repeated in the construction of these sacred objects (Exodus 35–40). It is notable that the ordination of Aaron and his sons is given in Leviticus 8–10 after the prescriptions of the sacrificial offerings (Leviticus 1–7). Upon the completion of the Tabernacle's construction, a cloud covers it completely as the Glory of the Lord enters, presumably from his previous domain above Mt. Sinai (Exodus 40:34). Yahweh is now intimately present in the midst of his people with purifying power that seeps into the community through the carefully refined performance of the hallowed rites. The well-being of the community rests entirely upon its center, which is, as it were, the center of the universe.

The Priestly Organization of Israel

The Tabernacle and all that goes with it is just half of the picture of this priestly model. The other half is a description of Israel as it was meant to be, standing in obedient relationship to its center. This part of the picture is found at the end of this epic narrative (Numbers 1:1–10:28), even as the Tabernacle comes at the beginning, the two parts forming an envelope figure around the levitical law (Leviticus).

One can hardly imagine a more highly integrated community than that of Israel gathered around the Tabernacle in the early chapters of Numbers. The priestly writers knew, like the scientific gurus of our computer-oriented society, that the concept of number is the fundamental factor in devising a comprehensive organization. The first act is taking a census of all Israel (everybody has a number . . . all the men, that is). Israel here is divided into the 12-tribe system, which facilitates the organizational structure. Tribal divisions are virtually ignored in the Book of Exodus. Israel acts and is addressed as a unit. The only tribal reference of significance is in the genealogy of Moses and Aaron (2:1; 6:14–25), assigning them to the tribe of Levi. This genealogy supports the priesthood of Aaron, his son Eleazar, and his grandson Phinehas, as the leading priests in the Tabernacle epic.

Although the Book of Exodus opens with a listing of the 12 tribes who go to Egypt, a list that includes Levi and Joseph, in the Book of Numbers, Levi is isolated from the other 12. These 12 include Ephraim and Manasseh in place of Joseph. The tribe of Levi has become the functioning priests of two orders: Aaron and his sons, who are the only designated "priests," and the "levites," who function as second-order priests. The transition from Levi's being a warlike tribe (Genesis 34:25f., 49:5–7) to the status of Temple servants, as we find them in Numbers 1:1–10:28, was a long one, one of many centuries, for this latter role belongs to the Second Temple of Ezra and Nehemiah. In between, they were a guild of priests at various shrines, as we find them in Deuteronomy and Judges 18–19. As the Tabernacle is symbolically a retroversion of the Temple, the Levites are similarly a projection back into this grand, wilderness, priestly, ideal schema.

In this grand scheme, the Tabernacle is the center, a center charged with electrical energy because the Lord resides in the Holy of Holies. Immediately surrounding it on three sides is the encampment of the Levites. On the east side, always the side of preference, are situated the priests. The priests perform the sacred rites. The Levites assist the priests. Together, in surrounding the Tabernacle, they guard against the other Israelites approaching this holy ground, for anyone outside these ordained functionaries who touches the sacred objects is to be put to death.

The 12 tribes are divided into four groups of three, each assigned to a specific side. Judah is on the east side, for only the tribe of Judah survived the kingdom, the Babylonian Exile, and the return to Jerusalem. It was the Second Temple community that this Tabernacle model served.

The entire camp of Israelites set out to journey to the plains of Moab, east of the land of Canaan and just north of the Dead Sea, according to our priestly model. The Lord signaled the time of march by lifting the cloud from the Tabernacle. There was a very detailed procedure for commencing the march. First, the priests covered all of the sacred objects. Then, the tribes on the east set out. Next, the Tabernacle was disassembled, the three divisions of Levites each being assigned very specific responsibilities in the operation. The two divisions that carried the parts of the Tabernacle proper then followed the first contingent of tribes. The tribes positioned on the south side went next. Then, the Kohathites, the Levites who were given the delicate task of carrying "the holy things"— the sacred objects that the priests had covered—followed. The task was delicate because they dare not touch the objects themselves or even look at them lest they die. Moreover, whereas the other Levites were given wagons to carry the Tabernacle, the Kohathites had to use poles and carry these objects on their shoulders. Behind the sacred objects came the tribes encamped on the west. Finally, the tribes situated on the north brought up the rear. The position of the priests in the march is not given.

All of the designated groups were numbered, that is, their men were numbered. The 12 tribes were numbered individually. The grand total of men 20 years old and older was 603,550. The numbers of the tribes are given a second time along with the totals of the groups of three positioned around the Tabernacle. The Levites are numbered according to the clans of the three sons of Levi, but here, all the males a month old and older are enrolled. The grand total of Levites was 22,000. The first-born Israelite males are numbered. Their grand total was 22,273. Cultic tradition assigned the first-born of humans and animals to the Lord. Here, the Lord accepts the Levites as substitutes for the first-born. But there are 273 more first-born Israelites than Levites. To compensate, the Lord allows five shekels for each of the extras to be paid to the priests according to the "shekel of the sanctuary." This is an obvious anachronism. To specify a unit of money defined by the temple, even prescribing the exchange of money by escapees in the desert, challenges credulity. It is not an historical narrative.

Six wagons and 12 oxen are given to the Levites to carry the Tabernacle and its accouterments. After the Tabernacle is set up, the tribes each bring offerings for the dedication of the altar, one day at a time. Each tribe presents the same offering and the list for each is given 12 times. The offering is as follows:

> *one silver plate weighing 130 shekels (about 3 1/4 pounds),*
> *one silver basin weighing 70 shekels, according to the*
> *shekel of the sanctuary, both of them full of choice flour*
> *mixed with oil for a grain offering; one golden dish weigh-*
> *ing 10 shekels, full of incense; one young bull, one ram,*
> *one male lamb a year old, for a burnt offering; one male*

goat for a sin offering; and for the sacrifice of well-being,
two oxen, five rams, five male goats, and five male lambs a
year old.[13]

If we examine this list in relation to the question of history or story, we must say that only the sheep and goats can be found in a desert environment. The flour, oil, bull, and oxen belong to an agricultural society. The gold and silver require a society of some wealth as well as the specialized means of creating these objects. This list may reflect some period of the Temple cult or it may represent the ideal cult according to the priestly writer.

The numbers also seem extravagantly large for a community in the desert. One would have to assume a total of two million persons that include 600,000 men 20 years old and older. The women and children are not mentioned. Thirteen thousand seven hundred Levites who transport the Tabernacle and its furnishings on six wagons is not only incongruous, it is preposterous, even though they are numbered from one month in age. It is interesting to note that the work life of the Levites is between ages 25 and 50. This, as well as the numbers, doesn't seem to fit a real world.

That the tribes all bring exactly the same offering is an indication that tribal differences do not count. Throughout the books of Exodus, Leviticus, and Numbers, there is a persistent three-tiered societal structure: the priests—Aaron and his sons—the Levites, and the Israelites. Exodus makes no mention of the tribes other than the 12 pillars, representing the 12 tribes (24:4) and the two craftsmen who make the sacred objects, one from the tribe of Judah and one from the tribe of Dan (31:2–6; 35:30–34). Moses' parents are of the "house of Levi" (2:1), but it is the priestly connection that counts. Curiously, his two sons are half Midianite. Jethro's influence is also seen in his suggestion of a system of judges that Moses adopts (Exodus 18). In all three books, there are several references to elders and a group of 70 elders (Exodus 24:1, 9; Numbers 11:16, 24–25) upon whom the spirit rests. But these functionaries play a minor role in comparison to the priests and Levites who dominate these three books.

Leviticus has only one reference to tribe. It records that the mother of a man who committed blasphemy belonged to the tribe of Dan (24:11).

There are numerous references to tribes in the Book of Numbers but except for chapter 32, which deals with the preparation for occupying the land, and chapter 36, which stipulates marriage within a tribe and inheritance, essentially the tribes are treated as 12 similar units of Israelites. The three-tiered structure dominates the book. A census of the 12 tribes is taken twice, at the outset of the wilderness journey (chapter 1) and after arriving in the plains of Moab (chapter 26). The 12 tribes bring their identical offerings for the dedication of the altar (chapter 7). They are divided into groups of three for camping around the Tabernacle and for the order of march (chapters 2 and 10). Representatives from each tribe are chosen to spy out the land (13:1–16). Moses speaks to the heads of the tribes (30:1). When they go to war against Midian, a thousand men are chosen from each tribe, showing again that the tribes are but categories without distinction. There is one discrepancy, however, in tribal identification. In the story of Aaron's staff budding almonds (chapter 17), Levi is counted as one of the 12 tribes. Elsewhere, the tribe of Levi is set apart as second-order priests. "They were not enrolled among the Israelites because there was no allotment given to them among the Israelites" (26:62). There really was an allotment, however, in the form of 48 towns scattered among the other tribes (35:6–8).

The Book of Leviticus

That the Book of Leviticus constitutes the center of the Tabernacle Theology is testimony to the priority of the priestly law that it contains. The name Leviticus does not refer to the Levites because they play no role in the book. They are mentioned only in passing with regard to the redemption of property in the cities of the Levites during the year of Jubilee (25:32–34). In Hellenistic times, the name referred to priestly law, and it is from the Septuagint that the title is derived,[14] as with those of all the Old Testament books. Moses is the mediator throughout the book, but there are a few times when the Lord speaks to Moses and Aaron together, once when the Lord speaks directly to Aaron and once to Aaron and his two sons. The ordinances apply either to the priests or the people of Israel, not to the Levites in particular.

The first 16 chapters are cultic law: detailed instructions on offering sacrifices, on the ordination of the priests, on clean and unclean persons and things, and on the Day of Atonement for the whole society. Chapters 17 through 26, commonly called the Holiness Code because of their emphasis on holiness, are a combination of cultic and ethical regulations culminating in the remarkable and unique idea of the year of Jubilee (chapter 25), when all land reverts to its original owners. Chapter 26 cites blessings or curses depending on obedience or disobedience. Chapter 27 is an appendix dealing with vows in the form of offerings to the Lord (i.e. to the sanctuary). Like most other bodies of law, Leviticus is a collection of earlier and later law, but in its present form, it seems to have been functional in the Second Temple period.

The Journey Tradition Continues

Following the conclusion of the Tabernacle Theology at Numbers 10:28, the remaining chapters of Numbers relate the journey through the wilderness, from Mt. Sinai to the plains of Moab. As others have observed in these chapters, law and narrative alternate.[15] There is, however, no necessary relation between them. The law might well have been a part of Leviticus for it belongs to the same priestly tradition.

The narratives cover a variety of themes attendant to the journey, including numerous conflicts within the community, especially challenging the leadership of Moses. The people complained about the lack of food. Manna had been introduced in Exodus 16 as "bread from heaven," which could not be kept more than one day except on the Sabbath, when it would not spoil. Aaron was told to keep a jar of it permanently in the sanctuary (16:33). In Numbers 11, quails drop all around the camp, as far as a day's journey on either side and about a yard deep (2 cubits). This is surely hyperbole, as the manna's functioning differently in natural and sacred circumstances is a theological device. Both examples appear to be literary expressions of the tenet that God provides repeatedly and abundantly. This is story, not history.

Moses is beleaguered on all sides. Not only must he deal with the grumbling Israelites but he has to defend them from the Lord's anger more than once. Aaron and Miriam criticize him for marrying a Cushite woman (probably a black woman). And even his right-hand man, Joshua, asks him to prevent Eldad and Medad from prophesying (11:28). A contingent of 250 Israelite men led by Korah and other Levites challenge the leadership of Moses and Aaron, even threatening the priesthood (chapter 16). The matter is settled when the Lord causes the earth to split open and swallow up these Levites and sends fire to consume the 250 men (16:35). When the whole congregation rebels against this treatment, the Lord sends a plague with the purpose of consuming them all. At this, Moses orders Aaron to take fire from the altar, adding incense to atone for the people, which stops the plague but not before 14,700 die (16:46–50). What a graphic picture of the power of the established cult to stem concerted human rebellion.

The congregation refuses to invade Canaan from the south, following the mixed report of the spies, and wants to choose a new leader and go back to Egypt. The Lord threatens to disinherit them, but Moses argues that it will be seen by the nations as a defeat and asks Him for their forgiveness. The Lord relents but condemns all of that generation except Caleb and Joshua to die in the wilderness. Hearing this, the Israelites decide to change their minds and invade Canaan, although Moses tells them it is too late, and they get driven back in defeat (chapters 13–14).

At one point, the patience of Moses wears thin. There is no water to be found. The Lord tells him to strike the rock and water will emerge. He does so, but begrudgingly. Consequently, his leadership is to end before the entrance into the land of Canaan (chapter 20). An equally consequential condition endangering the people's existence in the wilderness is the threat of poisonous serpents, which the Lord sends to bite them because of their obduracy. But then the Lord tells Moses to make a bronze serpent that has prophylactic powers in counteracting the poison (chapter 21). Perhaps these contradictory actions are intended to show that the people deserve punishment but that the Lord will achieve his purpose in spite of their faithlessness.

The complaint and rebellion narratives serve to show that in spite of the Israelites' obstinacy, the Lord provides for their needs and confirms the established cult and its leadership. The story of Balaam goes further in showing how inviolable are the Lord's intentions in bringing Israel to the land of Canaan. Balaam, in this story, is a Mesopotamian diviner who is hired at great expense by the Moabites and the Midianites to come to their territory and curse Israel. Divination was considered to be a powerful force in the ancient world and the curse had the power of the god who stood behind it. Curiously, it is the Lord who speaks to Balaam rather than one of the Babylonian gods. There is a deterministic ambiguity in the Lord's control over Balaam not unlike that of the poisonous serpents. The Lord tells Balaam to go with the elders of Moab and Midian but is also angry because he goes. This precipitates the delightful story of Balaam's donkey, which sees the angel of the Lord with drawn sword blocking the path and lies down. Balaam, lacking the vision of the donkey, beats it and the donkey speaks—in Hebrew! Balak, the king of Moab, takes Balaam to the high place of Baal, where some of Israel can be seen, and together they sacrifice a bull and a ram on each of seven altars in preparation for Balaam's curse against this advancing people. But he can only bless them. This scene is repeated twice. Israel has been blessed three times effusively. God's purpose in bringing them to Canaan is unremitting (22–24).

The remaining chapters of Numbers (25–36) focus on preparations for entering the land of Canaan. They represent a variety of concerns. There is apostasy: intermarriage with Moabites and Midianites, and Baal worship. Eleazar, Aaron's grandson, stems the tide and is awarded the perpetual priesthood (chapter 25). Here it should be noted that, while the Aaronic priesthood is predominant also in the Book of Joshua, it is unrecognized in the Books of Deuteronomy, Judges, Samuel, and Kings, except for a parenthetical reference in Judges 20:28, which smacks of a later addition.

There is concern about distribution of the land that will be occupied. This is the reason for the second census (chapter 26). The daughters of Zelophehad raise the question of the right of women to inherit property (27:1–11; 36). Limitations are imposed on women in making vows (30). After utterly destroying the Midianites, including Balaam, the distribution of booty between the army and the people is apportioned (31). The few remaining chapters (32–35) read as independent literary units but focus on the occupation of the land. Reuben, Gad, and half the tribe of Manasseh are to occupy land east of the Jordan, but they are to cross over with the other tribes to assist in the takeover of the land of Canaan (32). This is followed by a summary of the entire journey from Egypt to the plains of Moab with the exhortation to drive out the Canaanites (33). The boundaries of Canaan are designated along with the names of the tribal representatives who are to apportion the land for the remaining nine and a half tribes (34). The final step in the distribution of the land is the assignment of 48 cities for the Levites, scattered within the tribes, including the six cities of refuge for those who committed manslaughter unintentionally.

The momentum generated by the long journey described in Numbers 10:29 through chapter 36 would seem to lead directly to the Book of Joshua. The story of Balaam says essentially that no power on Earth will prevent the Lord from blessing Israel as his chosen nation (22–24). The unfolding plan of occupying the land of Canaan is the major emphasis of the chapters that follow (25–36). To be sure, the narratives on Joshua and the death of Moses in the miscellaneous chapters at the end of

Deuteronomy (31–34) form a bridge which continues the journey until the land is fully occupied at the end of Joshua 11. In terms of the continuity of the Journey Tradition, the Book of Deuteronomy is a hortatory and legal insert, a speech by Moses given just before the invasion of Canaan.

The Exodus, Tabernacle, and Journey traditions culminate in the Conquest tradition of Joshua that ends with Joshua 21. These four traditions have major common features and belong together. They constitute one story: how God liberated the people of Israel from the Egyptians, prescribed a priestly dominated cultic manner of life, led and provided for the community through a 40-year journey undergoing its spiritual formation, and overpowered all the inhabitants of Canaan through Israel's cultic faithfulness or corrected apostasy, until all the tribes were securely settled on their apportioned territory. As the narratives of the last chapters of Deuteronomy (32:44–52; 34) belong to this tradition, so the last two chapters of Joshua belong to the Deuteronomic tradition.

Story is History

These traditions, analyzed in the contexts in which they are found, are primarily story. History includes details that, on examination, are logical in their relatedness and consistent with what is known about the time and place from other sources. There is a sense, however, in which these stories are history. At the time when they were written, they represented reflections on the past, which became a significant part of the thought-world of that community of Hebrews or Jews. History is not just a matter of facts; it is a matter of thoughts. It is the thought-world of a given society that holds it together. Traditions are a combination of the past and present at the time of the writing, and they may be modified as they are transmitted.

The tradition of the Deliverance from Egyptian Bondage must have been written after a group of Hebrews who had been enslaved by Egyptians had become completely free from Egyptian authority but when the details had been largely forgotten. It was the deliverance as such that was prominent in the collective memory. And it had to be told in the most effective way. The fact that the only identification of the group(s) addressed by the Covenant Code is that they were "aliens in the land of Egypt" (Exodus 22:21; 23:9) tells us that this early agricultural society in Canaan treasured the memory of the "Deliverance." It was burned into their memory that God had freed them from enslave-ment. As the liberation was a collective experience so the memory of it crossed generations and took on perpetuation. It was a story to be cele-brated. It was story reflecting historical experience.

The Tabernacle Theology is also thought-history. It represents the thought-world of the post-exilic Second Temple, the temple of Ezra and Nehemiah. It may have been written by the society of priests in Babylon during the Exile as a model for a re-established community, or it may have been written in post-exilic Jerusalem. In either case, it utilized ear-lier traditions. The laws of Leviticus, especially of the Holiness Code, represent collections that accrued over a long period of time. The most elaborate prescripts appear to be the latest. Along with the priestly emphasis in the Books of Chronicles, the Tabernacle Theology was an enormously supportive tradition for the worship-centered community of the Second Temple. More will be said of this in our discussion of Chronicles-Ezra-Nehemiah in a proposed second volume.

The Journey Tradition is theological story that also served the Second Temple community as its historical thought-world. God was and is present in the community, leading it forward toward the Promised Land. Whereas the Tabernacle Theology portrays Israel as it ought to be, the Journey Tradition shows its seamy side. There is frequent com-plaint or contention. Food and drink are inadequate. The people are fearful of the inhabitants of Canaan. They rebel against the leadership of Moses and Aaron. They make a golden calf with Aaron's help. They cohabit with Moabites and Midianites, and serve the Baal of Peor. All of these indications of waywardness could be translated into analogous circumstances in the post-exilic community. In other words, the Journey Tradition served the leadership of that cultic-oriented society. It was part of the people's thought-history.

The stories and laws of Exodus-Leviticus-Numbers are so inter-twined with the whole range of Israel's historical experience from its earliest period to the time when this literature took on a final fixed form sometime in the post-exilic period that it is virtually impossible to speak of historical events in specific terms as motivating factors. Traditions are malleable. They are subject to modification as new realities or changing circumstances emerge. They also serve as modes of interpre-tation for ongoing change. History is the present view of the past.

What is central to all of these traditions, from beginning to end, is how God manifests Himself. Both in His lofty abode over Mt. Sinai, issuing the law that is to remain effective forever, and in His taberna-cling presence in the midst of the community, leading, protecting, chas-tising, purifying, God hovers over the world and over his people with sovereignty. The consciousness of God is compelling. There is no other power, no other good, none other worthy to be praised. Israel exists only because God has called him into being. This is the real story, fixed indelibly in the community memory. 📖

Notes

1. See below, chapter 5:106, 109.

2. James B. Pritchard, ed., *Ancient Near Eastern Texts,* 2nd ed. (Princeton: Princeton University Press, 1955), 119.

3. Avraham Biran, "Dan" in *Anchor Bible Dictionary,* 2:14.

4. Israel Finkelstein and Neil Asher Silberman, *The Bible Unearthed* (New York: The Free Press, 2001), 48–71.

5. Ibid., 59.

6. Pritchard, *ANET,* 378.

7. Amihai Mazar, *Archaeology of the Land of the Bible* (New York: Doubleday, 1990), 329–30.

8. Ibid., 330.

9. Brevard S. Childs, *The Book of Exodus* (Philadelphia: Westminster Press, 1974), 537–38.

10. G. Henton Davies, "Tabernacle" in *Interpreter's Dictionary of the Bible,* ed. George Arthur Buttrick (Nashville: Abingdon, 1962), 4:503.

11. Julius Wellhausen, *Prolegomena to the History of Ancient Israel* (New York: Meridian Books, 1957), 45.

12. Joshua R. Porter, "tabernacle" in *Harper's Bible Dictionary,* ed. Paul J. Achtemeier (San Francisco: Harper & Row, 1985), 1013–14.

13. Numbers 7:13-17.

14. Jacob Milgrim, *Leviticus 1-16* (New York: Doubleday, 1991), 1.

15. Jacob Milgrim, "Numbers" in *Anchor Bible Dictionary,* 4:1147–48.

Deuteronomy

Preface

The name Deuteronomy is a Greek word meaning second law. Apparently, it derives from verse 17:18, which in Hebrew speaks of the king writing for himself "a copy of this law," but which the Septuagint rendered "this second law," and the titles of the Old Testament books in English are taken from the Septuagint. Since the Code of Deuteronomy is significantly different from the earlier Covenant Code of Exodus 21–23, it is hard to know whether the Greek rendering was deliberate or a mistranslation.

Except for the last chapter, which is an account of Moses' death, and a few editorial comments about Moses, the book purports to be a series of speeches by Moses to the Israelites who are encamped east of the Jordan River in anticipation of their crossing over to the land of Canaan. From literary and historical analysis, we cannot read this as a literal account. There are many references in the text which point to later periods of Israelite history, some suggesting one era and others other eras. The text, it appears, is to some extent a collection and to some extent an amalgam, having served, in the process of its history, several Israelite communities successively over the period from the early northern settlement to post-exilic Judah at the time(s) of Ezra and Nehemiah. Consequently, the historical setting of the book, in my view, is story. But the text in its portions reflects history. Laws reflect a real society, and to characterize that society is to recognize history.

One prominent theme in much of the homiletical material is the gift of the land to Israel, the Lord giving them the power to defeat and destroy the nations dwelling there (7:1-6, 17-26; 8:19-20; 9:1-7; 11:22-25; 12:29-32; 19:1, 8-9; 25:17-19). In contrast, in the strictly legal material, the Ammonites and Moabites are denied admission to the assembly of the Lord, but nothing is said about harming or displacing them. More liberally, the Edomites and Egyptians are to be shown respect, the third generation born to them even admitted to the assembly of the Lord (23:3, 7-8). These are surely different sources with distinctly different points of view, the former being idealistic and indifferent to historical realities. Had Israel killed off all the indigenous peoples, assuming that it could, there would have been no conflict with them in later generations. War was certainly common and brutal, but as with the Book of Joshua, where archaeological evidence denies the historicity of the account, the barbarous demands of the Lord in Deuteronomy to kill off whole towns and peoples should be seen as the ardor of zealous theologians.

Contents

The Book of Deuteronomy begins with the statement: "These are the words that Moses spoke to all Israel beyond the Jordan—in the wilderness . . ."

Long ago, it was observed that the writer of these words was in the land of Canaan, focusing eastward on the hills of Moab. This observation was one of the early clues that undermined the traditional belief that Moses wrote the Pentateuch, for at the end of Deuteronomy, Moses is said to have died east of the Jordan River. Even the early rabbis, who assigned the authorship of the Pentateuch to Moses in the Talmud, attributed the last eight verses of Deuteronomy, the account of Moses' death, to Joshua.

The first five verses are editorial, introducing the opening speech of Moses that concludes at 4:40, following which is a brief appendix where Moses selects three cities of refuge east of the Jordan. The speech, itself, is largely a brief summary of the journey from Mt. Sinai to the banks of the Jordan River, as found in Numbers with references to the Sinai experience in Exodus. There is also allusion to an exile, reflecting either that of the northern tribes to Assyria or of Judah to Babylon (4:25-31).

The style of this as well as of the other speeches of Moses in Deuteronomy is emphatically hortatory. This alone sets Deuteronomy apart from the other books of Moses, but there are also major differences in content.

The second speech of Moses embraces the bulk of the book (5–28). Like the first speech, it is preceded by a five-verse editorial introduction (4:44–48). And like the Sinai Event in Exodus, it begins with the Ten Commandments, recalling their reception at Mt. Horeb. However, Moses identifies the Israel whom he is addressing on the plain east of the Jordan River with the Israel who surrounded the mountain. "Not with our ancestors did the Lord make this covenant, but with us, who are all of us here alive today" (5:3).

When is "today" in this passage? Where is "here?" And is it the Israel standing before Moses east of the Jordan River who is really being addressed? The literal translation of the last half of this verse in Hebrew is: "but with us, we, these here today, all of us living."

The verse as a whole has an existential character. The author is not really denying that the Lord made a covenant with the Israel who stood before Mt. Horeb 40 years ago. Indeed, the same Ten Commandments as those of Exodus 20, with slight modification, are given here, followed by a description of the experience of those who stood around the mountain. But the experience is related with such passion that the awful presence of God is transmitted to the reader. The past becomes a living present. The context recognizes the immense power attendant to the covenant given in its inception, but verse 5:3 emphasizes its present reality. The covenant is for the living and that means every generation.

The core of the second address of Moses is the strictly legal section, chapters 12–26, commonly called the Code of Deuteronomy. The chapters leading up to it are filled with persuasion, exhortation, and admonishment to live by these laws. The emphasis in these chapters is on the complete devotion to the Lord (Yahweh). The land of Canaan, about to be occupied, is God's gift to Israel. The inhabitants of Canaan are to be destroyed. There must be no collaboration with them, no intermarriage, and every aspect of their religion must be annihilated. As Israel has been sustained by God throughout the wilderness journey, he will bless them with abundance if they are fully faithful in obeying these commandments.

At the end of the Code, there is a chapter of laws, chapter 27, which seems to be unrelated to the Code but which has the same provenance.

The geographical references in this chapter as well as the consequences in terms of the blessing and the curse are the same as those found in the material that just precedes and thus introduces the Code (11:29–30). All of these laws are said to be associated with the sanctuary at Shechem.

Like the chapters that introduce the Code, the conclusion of Moses' second address, chapter 28, argues strongly for Israel's dedicated commitment to these laws. Indeed, this longest chapter of the book deals only with the consequences of obedience or disobedience, blessings or curses. And there are nearly four times as many curses as blessings.

This extensive condemnation in the form of the curses, especially the last half of them (verses 47–68), are descriptive of the experience of exile and suggest that they were written as a reflection of the fall of the Northern Kingdom in 722 BCE, when substantial numbers of Israelites were transported to the regions of Assyria, or after the fall of Jerusalem (586 BCE), when numerous Judaeans were taken to Babylon.

The third speech of Moses, chapters 29 and 30, further amplifies the blessings and curses in chapter 28. Whether or not 29:1 in the English versions is the beginning of this third address or is the conclusion of chapter 28 is uncertain because it is numbered 28:69 in the Hebrew text. But chapter 30 emphasizes the compassion of the Lord in restoring the fortunes of his people unlike the end of chapter 28, which emphasizes exile as God's judgment. It appears that exile has occurred at the time when chapter 30 was written. Moses' third address reads like a supplement to chapter 28.

The remaining four chapters of Deuteronomy describe Moses' final acts and words, anticipating his death. He acts with magnanimity as a great leader would do. He summons Joshua and together they stand before the tent of meeting where the Lord appears in a pillar of cloud and ordains Joshua to succeed Moses as leader. He writes down the law and gives it to the Levites, telling them to place it beside the ark of the covenant. But he admonishes them, saying he knows that after his death, they will act corruptly and trouble will befall them.

The Song of Moses (32:1–43) is a testimonial which comes fittingly after the extensive exhortation, predicted degeneracy, and restoration. Its scope is vast and sweeping and it exudes great passion. When God established the nations, he chose Jacob to be Yahweh's people even as—so this text says—he assigned gods to the other nations. Yahweh nourished Israel richly but Israel rebelled. For this, Yahweh seethes in anger and wants to utterly destroy his people, but that would make his enemies triumph. So he will destroy his enemies and restore his people. It is a poem of moving power, a tour de force, a heroic conclusion to the fervent discourse of persuasion to live by the Code. This is surely one of the pre-eminent poems in the whole Old Testament. It could have served—and may have at one time—as the conclusion to the Book of Deuteronomy as a whole.

This Song of Moses was undoubtedly an independent psalm that was placed here because it fit. It does not mention the law, only Yahweh's creative power and Jacob's waywardness (the name Israel is not used). The only geographical term is Bashan, the rich agricultural area east of the Sea of Galilee and part of the territory occupied early on by the people known as Jacob or Israel. Nothing relates it to the rest of Deuteronomy in particular. It simply tells a story about God and his people that is told over and over again throughout the Old Testament. It is probably an early poem since there is no reference to a political or religious institution. It could be from the time of Moses, even from Moses himself.

As the Song of Moses was added to the Book of the Law (chapters 12–26), with the passionate entreaty to live by it that both precedes and follows (chapters 5–11, 27–31), another old poem, the Blessing of Moses (chapter 33) is also an appendix. It, also, has no relation to the Code but it is an entirely different poem. Whereas the Song of Moses is primarily story—theological story—the Blessing of Moses is a form of history. But it is history known to the Deuteronomic tradition, which has a northern orientation. Joseph is the leading tribe with Ephraim and Manasseh as major subdivisions. Levi is the priesthood throughout the land. Judah here is a minor tribe and seems to be in trouble. Archaeological findings show sparse settlement in Judah in the Iron Age I (1150–900 BCE), the inhabitants having come from the north.[1] Reuben, east of the Jordan, also is threatened. Simeon is not mentioned here, although it is listed as one of the 12 tribes in 27:12–13. All of the other tribes are described as prosperous. This poem portrays the Israel of the north as blessed by the Lord.

The two prose passages at the end of the book (32:44–52; 34) recount the final days of Moses. They pick up the narrative from the end of chapter 31 with a sense of continuity such that the two long poems discussed above appear to be insertions. Moses finishes admonishing Israel to live by "this law." Then the Lord tells him to ascend Mt. Nebo to view the whole land that Israel will occupy.

Moses has fulfilled his mission. He dies and is mourned for 30 days. Joshua succeeds him.

Provenance

For nearly 200 years, biblical scholars have identified the "book of the law" found in the temple of Jerusalem during its renovation by King Josiah as an early edition of the Book of Deuteronomy (II Kings 22:8–10). The description of Josiah's reform of the entire religious establishment of Judah on the basis of that book so closely reflects the demands of Deuteronomy that they fit together like hand and glove (II Kings 23). Josiah cleansed the temple and all Jerusalem of idolatrous worship. He destroyed the high places and their cult objects, not only in Judah, but also in Samaria. Jerusalem was then the only legitimate place to keep the Passover, which he renewed, its being identified with Deuteronomy's repeated phrase: "the place that the Lord your God will choose out of all your tribes as his habitation to put his name there." (12:5).

How did the Book of Deuteronomy come to be in the temple in Jerusalem? Jerusalem is not to be found in the book, and of the three places where Judah is mentioned, two are tangential and the third is in the Blessing of Moses discussed above. All of the geographical references are to places either east of the Jordan River or in northern Israel. Two stipulations are given regarding the positioning of this law. In chapter 27, large stones are to be set up on Mt. Ebal. They are to be covered with plaster and the law is to be written upon them (verses 2–4). In 31:24–26, the Levites are to place "this book of the law . . . beside the ark." Twice (11:29–30; 27:12–13), the blessing and the curse are to be placed on Mt. Gerizim and Mt. Ebal, respectively. In the first instance, there is added, "beside the oak of Moreh," which indicates Shechem (Genesis 12:6). While the Book of Deuteronomy has been edited in the ongoing process of its transmission, the bulk of the Code—the strictly legal portion (12–26)—must be assigned to the major shrines in northern Israel: certainly Shechem; very likely Shiloh, where the ark was for some period (I Samuel 4:3; Jeremiah 7:12); Bethel, where the ark is reported to have been kept for a time (Judges 20:27–28) in spite of its and Dan's excoriation by the Deuteronomic editor (I Kings 12:29). The Code may have been actively utilized also in Dan with its priesthood of the line of Moses (Judges 18:30). There is no reason to deny a core of the Code of Deuteronomy, the ordinances governing a small-town rural society, to Moses as author. The book in its present form appears to be a composite: an initial core that accumulated numerous additions as it served different constituencies of Israel.

As to how an early edition of this book came to Jerusalem, many scholars hold that it was brought there after the fall of the Northern Kingdom in 721 BCE. Archaeology has shown "that suddenly, at the end of the 8th century BCE, Jerusalem underwent an unprecedented population explosion . . . Jerusalem was transformed from a modest highland town of about 10 or 12 acres to a huge urban area of 150 acres of closely packed houses, workshops, and public buildings."[2] To explain this influx, it is theorized that there was a mass migration from the Northern Kingdom when the Assyrians conquered Samaria. Subsequently, Hezekiah, who came to the throne in 715 BCE, initiated a widespread religious reform, eradicating the high places of the pagan cults and instituting a Yahweh-only program (II Kings 18:3–6). While there is no evidence that the Book of Deuteronomy was a factor in this reform, there is a strong compatibility between them. That is as much as we can say.

The devotees of Yahweh gave high praise to Hezekiah for his reform but the political consequences were a disaster. Judah had become a vassal of Assyria under Hezekiah's father, Ahaz. This meant that the state religion of Assyria had to be practiced there. For Hezekiah to throw out the foreign cults, therefore, was to proclaim independence. Consequently, Sennacherib brought his army into Judah, subdued all the fortified cities—his own account says 46—and levied heavy tribute on the land.

Hezekiah's son, Manasseh, reversed course and brought back the Canaanite and foreign cults. His reign was long and stable. At the end of it, however, Assyria had weakened and was fighting for survival. This allowed Josiah to risk reform again without jeopardy. We do not know when or how an edition of Deuteronomy found its way into the temple of Jerusalem, but that it did seems to be the case. And while it may not have been the impetus for that reform, it provided strong support, witness Josiah's reaction when he heard the book read (II Kings 22:11–13).

It is fair to say that some form of the Book of Deuteronomy served several different communities of Israel: initially northern Israel, then Judah under Hezekiah, then Jerusalem under Josiah, and it surely was part of the law book that Ezra read to post-Exilic Israel (Nehemiah

8:1–3). It is our assumption that in each of these communities, some new material was added or what had been handed down was modified to serve the interests of that particular community.

To illustrate this, a leading theme in the Code relates to the place of worship, whether for sacrifice, vows and offerings, observing the festivals, or the tithe. Emphasis is placed on these observances happening only "at the place that the Lord your God will choose." This statement occurs 21 times in the Code (12–26) and once in chapter 31. No name is associated with "the place." In nine of those passages, the phrase "as a dwelling for his name" or "to put his name there" is added. In two instances, early in the Code (12:5, 14), a specific place seems to be intended without being named. In 12:5, the phrase "out of all your tribes" is added, and in 12:14 "in one of your tribes." The editor of the Books of Kings identifies "the place" as "Jerusalem, the city where I have chosen to put my name" (I Kings 11:36).

Given the kind of reforms instituted by Hezekiah and Josiah, there is no doubt that Jerusalem was the only legitimate place to worship during their reigns. However, Jeremiah identifies "Shiloh, where I made my name dwell at first," as a northern forerunner of the name theology (7:12). But it is unlikely that Shiloh was singular as a legitimate place of worship in the North. Deuteronomy 27 prescribes the building of an altar to Yahweh on Mt. Ebal where sacrifices are to be offered (verses 5–7). Mt. Ebal overlooks the city of Shechem. It is mentioned along with Mt. Gerizim—on the other side of Shechem—for witnessing the curse and the blessing of this law, both in 11:29 and 27:12–13, the signs of obedience and disobedience. The parallel law in the earlier Covenant Code in Exodus demands, similarly, that the altar be made of unhewn stone but suggests multiple altars: "in every place where I cause my name to be remembered I will come to you and bless you" (Exodus 20:24–25). The German scholar Gerhard von Rad estimates that about 50 percent of the laws in Deuteronomy have parallels in the Covenant Code (Exodus 20:22–23:19[3]). The parallel law regarding the altar of unhewn stone is in Deuteronomy 27:6. Also, the law forbidding having a stone pillar or a sacred pole "beside the altar that you make for the Lord your God" (Deuteronomy 16:21) hardly presumes to be a central shrine. It is obviously a common altar.

Three yearly festivals are to be celebrated at "the place that the Lord your God will choose": Passover, Weeks, and Booths (16:1–17). Of these, the date is prescribed only for Passover—the new moon of the spring month Abib (16:1). This is also referred to as the Festival of Unleavened Bread, a seven-day observance ending with "a solemn assembly" (according to the Masoretic text), a ritual occasion different from the assembly referred to in 23:1–8 that apparently served political purposes. Both the Septuagint and the Samaritan Pentateuch have the festival end with a feast instead (16:8).

The other two festivals are not determined by the calendar but by the season. The Feast of Weeks comes seven weeks after the beginning of the grain harvest, and the Feast of Booths comes at the end of the vintage harvest (16:9–17). The dates would vary somewhat each year, but there would also be a staggering of observances from south to north because the growing year would gradually come later as it moved north. These were celebrations of the householders' families, including slaves, and also all others in the towns who were not landholders: Levites, orphans, widows, and strangers were to be included. There were two Thanksgivings with no one left out.

The passages which refer to an altar or a "place" for the worship of Yahweh seem to reflect a variety of circumstances: common altars, major shrines, or a singular designated shrine. Given the indications that suggest the historical transition of Deuteronomy from its original home in the north to Judah at the time of Hezekiah and then, after going underground during Manasseh's reign, becoming the constitution for Josiah's theocracy, one may theorize that the book, itself, adapted to such changing circumstances. However, the modifications and accretions represent a far too complex process to identify. The German historian Martin Noth presented the enticing theory that the first three chapters of Deuteronomy are an introduction, not only to the rest of this book, but to what has become known as the Deuteronomistic History: Joshua, Judges, Samuel, and Kings. While the influence of Deuteronomy on these historical books is widely recognized, the homiletical style of the first three chapters fits consistently and uniquely with that of so much of the rest of the book.[4] We are led to believe that the structure of Deuteronomy is composite.

In recent years, it has been observed that the form of Deuteronomy bears striking resemblance to some international suzerainty treaties, especially those known of the Hittites from the Late Bronze Age (1550–1200 BCE) and of the Assyrians of the 7th century BCE. George Mendenhall, in the 1950s, found a common outline in the Hittite treaties, the elements of which can be seen in the framework of

Deuteronomy (chapters 1–11 and 27–34; following the designation of Adam Welch). The structure is as follows:

- ▸ Identification of the Covenant Giver—the graciousness of the suzerain toward the vassal and the exclusive fidelity due the former from the latter
- ▸ The Historical Prologue—all that the suzerain has given the vassal in the past
- ▸ The Stipulations—what is required of the vassal
- ▸ The Provision for Deposit and Periodic Public Reading
- ▸ The List of Witnesses to the Treaty
- ▸ The Blessings and Curses
- ▸ The Ratification Ceremony
- ▸ The Imposition of the Curses[5]

Mendenhall says that these elements were common to treaties in the Near-East of the Late Bronze Age but in their cultural adaptation, they assumed patterns of their own. In Deuteronomy 6, the identification of the Covenant Giver, "Hear, O Israel: The Lord is our God, the Lord alone," is linked to what God has done for Israel, namely, delivered them from Egypt.[6] The Stipulations are the Ten Commandments (Deuteronomy 5). There is to be a public reading before all Israel every seventh year (31:10–13) and the law is to be deposited beside the ark (31:26). Witnesses in the Late Bronze Age treaties are the gods, which have no place in monotheistic Israel. The blessings and lengthy curses are spelled out in chapter 28. Mendenhall finds a ratification ceremony in chapter 27, where the 12 tribes affirm the curses, read by the Levites in a cultic observance at Shechem.[7]

Moshe Weinfeld finds close parallels between the vassal treaties of Esarhaddon and the framework to the Code of Deuteronomy, especially in chapters 28 and 29. Deuteronomy, like these vassal treaties, he says, is really "a loyalty oath imposed by the sovereign on his vassal,"[8] the sovereign being Yahweh and the vassal being Israel. These treaties belong to the 7th century BCE. He recognizes the influence on Deuteronomy of both the Hittite and Assyrian models.[9] However, because the Esarhaddon treaties are so militaristic and threatening, while lacking several features of the Hittite models, Mendenhall assesses them as having no more than minor influence on the writing of Deuteronomy in relation to that of the Hittite treaties.[10]

What is to be learned from these discoveries is that the scribes who wrote or edited the framework to the Code of Deuteronomy were knowl-edgeable about the forms of international covenants. (The Hebrew word for treaty is the same as the word for covenant.) Further, it is apparent that scribes were participants, to some degree, in the creation of the narrative. If Mendenhall's analysis is correct, the bulk of the substance of this material is earlier rather than later. He thinks the blessings and curses in Deuteronomy 27 may go back to the time of Moses in Transjordan. On the other hand, the extended curses in chapter 28, with descriptions of deprivation and exile constituting the last half of this long chapter, suggest the experience of the Babylonian Exile (597–538 BCE). It may be inferred that this material was added during that Exile. It is misleading, therefore, for Weinfeld to say that Deuteronomy is to be dated in the 7th century BCE.[11] Undoubtedly, there was a 7th-century edition, but there is much in the book that points to earlier periods and the material in chapter 28 makes the text as it now stands at least as late as the Babylonian Exile. As we said before, Deuteronomy is a composite of writings from as early, perhaps, as the time of Moses in the 13th or 12th century BCE down to the Exile or later. Much of the Code, however, we would assign to the early settlement in the north. In particular, the singular section about the king suggests a strong reaction against Solomon (17:14–20). This would point to the time of Jeroboam I, when the society was in a formative period (after 922 BCE).

The Society Served by the Code

One way of searching for the earliest edition of Deuteronomy is to examine the laws apart from the homiletical material. The laws themselves should reveal the kind of society that they served. All of the laws are included in the Code and the appended old law of chapter 27. Commonly, the Code is considered to be chapters 12–26 and 28, although chapter 28 has no law; it has only blessings and curses.

Chapter 27 begins with a reference to Moses in the third person. Indeed, this is found not only in verse 1 but in verses 9 and 11. These introductions indicate separate units. One must hasten to add, however, that the Code as a whole is a collection of laws that are not organized in a particular order, although one can find sections of laws within a specific category. Chapters 12–16 deal mostly with cult and worship; chapters 17–20 relate primarily to offices and institutions. Chapter 27 presents a sense of conclusion to the entire collection, calling for the laws to be written on plastered stones to be set up on Mt. Ebal and an altar to be built beside them. The list of curses at the end of the chapter is related to half the tribes standing on Mt. Ebal for the curse and half of them standing on Mt. Gerizim for the blessing, a theme that appears just before the beginning of the Code (11:29), forming an envelope figure to the collection. Nevertheless, the end of the Code can also be seen in the concluding statement at the end of chapter 28 in Hebrew. (The English translators, in my view, have mistakenly made it an introduction to chapter 29.) "These are the words of the covenant that the Lord commanded Moses to make with the Israelites in the land of Moab, in addition to the covenant that he had made with them at Horeb." To have more than one conclusion suggests the process of an evolutionary growth of the text.

The Code is said to begin with chapter 12 because of its introductory statement, which is not unlike the concluding statement just noted. "These are the statutes and ordinances that you must diligently observe in the land that the Lord, the God of your ancestors, has given you to occupy all the days that you live on the earth." The first two chapters, however, exhibit the same passionate hortatory style as found in the preceding chapters 4–11. This is preached law. It is an elaboration with some particulars of the theme found in chapter 7:1–6. There is to be no fraternization with the peoples of the land. Every form of their religion is to be annihilated. Every aspect of Yahweh worship is to be held at "the place that the Lord your God will choose out of all your tribes as his habitation to put his name there" (12:5). Only in chapter 12 is "the place" designated in particular, though unnamed.

If the hortatory material common to chapters 4 through 13 comes from writers associated with the reforms of Hezekiah or Josiah, Jerusalem then becomes inferred as "the place" in chapter 12. However, as we know from the books of Kings, especially the Elijah narratives, the challenge which the Canaanite religion posed to the Yahweh cult in the north was so threatening and intense that this hortatory material could well be seen as a reaction to that challenge. Whether this material represents original writing or a revision of previous tradition is beyond our ability to determine. It is apparent, however, that beginning with chapter 14, the laws are presented in a more straightforward manner, not attended by the exhortation which betrays a tension over obedience to the law.

What is so appealing about the Code of Deuteronomy is that it is a program for life in community. It is addressed to the people, often more specifically to the heads of households, using such language as "you and your households together" (12:7) and "you together with your son and your daughter, your male and female slaves" (12:18). The law about buying and releasing a Hebrew slave can only be understood as being addressed to a householder (15:12–17). Many of the laws are generic, such as those distinguishing between clean and unclean animals and fish for food (14:1–20). A puzzling feature of the Book of Deuteronomy found both in the legal and homiletical material is the seemingly arbitrary use of the second person singular and plural pronouns. Unfortunately, the English language no longer distinguishes between the two, so this cannot be seen in translation. Attempts have been made to separate literary sources on this basis, but they turn out to be too interdependent. Moreover, the Septuagint often varies the use of these forms from those in the Masoretic Text.[12] The most reasonable explanation of this phenomenon, in my view, is that it is a device that serves to unite the individual and the community. Just as the focus is sometimes on the individual as a class, as noted above, and sometimes on the people as a whole, the usage of the pronouns has a unifying effect.

The elders were the householders or the most prominent of them. In each town, they made decisions affecting the community at large. They appointed judges to handle legal decisions and officials to administer town functions (16:18). The Levites were the priests stationed in each town. They were members of a guild identified as the tribe of Levi. They were given certain portions of the sacrifices and the first fruits when they functioned at the shrine (18:3–4), and in the towns, they received portions of the third-year tithe (14:28–29). They may have had some income from other sources (18:8; the Hebrew is obscure).

The case of the homicide found somewhere near the border of two adjoining townships is instructive (21:1–9). The elders and the judges from each town measure the distance from the body to their town. The town closest to the body is responsible. It must be absolved of blood guilt. The elders bring a heifer to the place, break its neck, and confess their innocence. The Levites absolve them. The onus is on the elders, who represent their community. A similar case is that of the unruly son who is beyond the control of his parents. He is brought to the gate of the town where the elders stone him to death (21:18–21).

There is no royal theology in Deuteronomy. Indeed, the king is portrayed as a subordinate figure in the only passage about him in the book (17:14–20). First of all, he must be a member of the community "whom the Lord your God will choose." What does this mean in practical terms? Who chose the king? In the abundant material about northern Israel in the Books of Kings, it was the prophets who made and unmade kings. The prophets were the political arm of Yahweh. This passage could not have been written in Judah because the Davidic dynasty reigned there.

There are only two passages in Deuteronomy where prophets are discussed. In 13:1–5, prophets who attempt to lead the people to worship other gods are to be put to death. In 18:15–22, the Lord will raise up a prophet like him, Moses, who will speak on behalf of the Lord, but any prophet who speaks in the name of other gods should die. This certainly reflects the divided society of the Northern Kingdom. The Elijah and Micaiah narratives in I Kings 17–22 portray the intense conflict between the Baal prophets and the Yahweh prophets. The first two chapters of the Code, 12–13, reflect the same severe threat from the Canaanite cults to the community of Yahweh. No doubt, the same religious situation is addressed, but we cannot link the particulars.

While the prophets in the North may have had some role in the selection of the king, as Samuel did in choosing Saul and David in Judah, the law is directed to the community and the elders who governed at the local level. There is a clear and antagonistic inference about Solomon. The king must not "return the people to Egypt in order to acquire more horses," meaning to enslave the people while cultivating his horse trading enterprise. He must not acquire many wives or much silver and gold. This reference suggests that it was written shortly after the breakup of the united monarchy, probably in the reign of Jeroboam the first.

The king is not to exalt himself above his people. He shall be subject to this law. Nothing is said about his duties. This is a very unusual description of a king, and it reflects the tenor of the entire Code, if not the book as a whole. The focus is on the well-being of the community as a whole. Special attention is given to those who are vulnerable. The third-year tithe is a public store for resident aliens, orphans, and widows as well as for the Levites, whose means of support is the public dole (14:28–29). Those who are well off are enjoined to give liberally to the poor (15:7–11). For those who are deep in debt, the institution of slavery provides the means of survival. They sell themselves and their family members to a landowner for basic needs for a period of seven years, after which the debt is wiped out and enough capital is given to the bankrupt family to start again (15:1–6, 12–18). The hungry are allowed to enter a field or vineyard to eat from the crops there but not to take anything out (23:24–25). The farmer is to leave behind gleanings of his crops for the alien, the orphan, and the widow (24:19–22). All of those dependent on public support are invited to go to the central shrine for the festivals of weeks and booths along with the householder families, including the slaves (16:9–15).

The disfranchised are further protected from abuse. The same standard of justice is to be accorded aliens. A widow's garment is not to be taken in pledge (24:17), and that of a poor person taken as collateral cannot be kept overnight. Indeed, the lender is not allowed to enter the domain of the borrower for the pledge (24:10–13). Most remarkable, perhaps, is the obligation not to return slaves to their owners (23:15–16).

There were laws protecting women from being exploited. While adultery was punishable by death for both parties, even for an engaged woman who consented, the rape of a betrothed woman punished only the man with the same severity. The rape of a virgin who was not engaged demanded unbroken marriage with her plus a hefty fine paid to her father. A newly married man who, out of dislike for his wife, charged that she was not a virgin was subject to her parents producing what apparently was the cloth containing her last menstruation before marriage as evidence (22:13–29). If this was done, the man had to pay double the fine of the rape of an unattached virgin. If the evidence was lacking, she was to be stoned to death. While in modern terms, some of these measures are hardly relief from exploitation, they represent protection from abuse according to ancient standards. Even a captive woman had such protection (21:10–14). And in the case of a man having two wives, one loved and the other unloved, where the firstborn is the son of the unloved, his status could not be changed (21:15–17).

Deuteronomy modified the practice of blood revenge common to the ancient world. Those who murdered with intent were, indeed, given into the hands of the victim's family to exact retribution (19:11–13). But in the case of someone who caused a death accidentally, he could flee to one of the three cities of refuge for protection. The land was divided into three regions for this purpose (19:2–3). Prosecution of a crime depended on witnesses. There had to be two or three for a charge to be sustained. A single witness could initiate a trial after which both parties had to appear at the shrine before priests and judges. The judges were to investigate. If the charge could not be sustained, the one who brought it was given the penalty (19:15–21). The presence of the priest was probably intended to promote veracity. There was also a limitation imposed on corporal punishment (25:1–3).

Unlike the later priestly legislation, the Code of Deuteronomy does not promote an exclusively Hebrew community, although it is selective. The third generation of Edomites and Egyptians—presumably those who have integrated into the community—could be admitted to the assembly of the Lord (23:7–8), but Ammonites and Moabites were rejected (23:3–6), as reflected in the story of Lot's daughters (Genesis 19:30–37). The assembly of the Lord would have been the gathering of elders, who were the governing body at the local level. The Egyptians were given this status in recognition of the Israelites having been aliens in their land, irrespective of the numerous references throughout Deuteronomy about the slavery in Egypt. The Edomites were said to be brothers, suggesting either a time before the enormous hostility against them developed or their acceptance in the north while being shunned in the south.

The family and the town were the basic social units. There was no legislation pertaining to the tribe; in fact, the tribe as a social unit is not even recognized in the Code, apart from the special case of the Levites who were really a guild. The wife of a man who died without leaving a son was not to marry outside that family. It was the husband's brother's duty to marry her and raise up an heir for the deceased. If he refused, the social pressure on him from the entire town made him a pariah (25:5–10). Concern for the community as a whole was stressed. Interest on loans to other Israelites was forbidden (23:19–20). Neighbors were enjoined to care for each other's strayed animals and lost items, and to assist any animals in difficulty (22:1–4). Landmarks were not to be moved. A revealing comment, "set up by former generations," suggests that Israelites had settled on the land much earlier than the time purported in the writing (19:14). This law is also one of the 12 curses in the old law code of chapter 27.

Punishment, from our perspective, was severe. Death was meted out for disloyalty in cultic or sexual commitments. It was commitment to Yahweh that united the people of Israel and gave them a pattern of life suitable for their well-being. It was the sexual mores that stabilized the family and the community, channeling those emotions into proper relationships for the birth and care of ongoing generations. The murderer, the diviner, the unruly son were also major threats to the society and subject to capital punishment. The survival of the community of Israel was at stake.

There is much about war in Deuteronomy. It is obvious, however, that the military conflicts that engaged Israel were regional. "You shall annihilate them—the Hittites and the Amorites, the Canaanites and the Perizzites, the Hivites and the Jebusites—just as the Lord your God has commanded" (20:17). A number of relatively small ethnic groups were competing for ownership in the land of Canaan. War was an ever-present phenomenon. As Yahweh demanded strict controls within Israel, he was equally zealous in empowering the armies of Israel in defeating their enemies and expanding their territory. It must be admitted, however, that Yahweh's might is presented idealistically, especially in chapter 20, where every man who does not wish to fight may return home. The stipulations always assume that Israel will win. This does raise questions about whether or not the war statements reflect the reality of the northern Israelite settlement or later theological editing.

Gerhard von Rad refers to the war theology of Deuteronomy as the Holy War.[13] "Deuteronomy is the one corpus in the Old Testament containing numerous laws about war, regulations about the investment of cities, prisoners of war, etc. at the back of which stand traditions which are without doubt old."[14] He sees layers of tradition that are both older and younger. On the one hand, it is not tribal action of an earlier period that is assumed but later Israel as a unit. On the other hand, the king's normal involvement is not given, suggesting an earlier period.[15] What von Rad does not consider, however, is the possibility that Israel was a people before there were tribal divisions and before there was a king. It must be remembered that there was a people known as Israel noted on the Stele of Merneptah, dated at the end of the 13th century BCE. Israel was recognized as a people long before there was a kingdom and long before the tribes were unified, if indeed they ever were unified. All that is said about Israel in this Stele is that they were defeated by Merneptah, but they seem to be located in the hill country of central Canaan.[16] This is also where the Israel in Deuteronomy was situated.

Conclusion

What is so appealing about the Book of Deuteronomy is that it is a program for a just and humane society, where the seat of authority was in the hands of those who were responsible for its social, political, and economic well-being. It was the elders, the heads of families, the landowners who made decisions in the public interest on the basis of these laws. Israel was composed of small towns supported by an agricultural economy. It was united by a common faith in Yahweh through whose law all members of the society were to be treated with respect. The king was not to exalt himself but was to be subject to the law like everyone else. The disadvantaged were to be cared for both by social legislation and altruistic concern. Provision was made for families who experienced disaster to be in servitude for a limited time to whose who prospered and then to be given a fresh start.

The Levites as cultic practitioners were independent of political authority but dependent upon the elders for their sustenance. They were teachers and interpreters of religious functions. They served also as physicians (24:8) and chaplains in the army (20:2–4). While those stationed at the shrines performed some cultic functions for which certain portions of the sacrificial animals were given to them (18:3–5), the town Levites simply joined the local families in the celebrations of the festivals like the orphans and the widows. Unlike the priestly legislation in Exodus through Numbers, there is no description of how the Levites functioned in ritual other than the single reference showing the priest taking the basket of first fruits and setting it down before the altar (26:4).

There were judges in the towns who held court and made decisions in civil cases (16:18–20). They had investigative functions (19:15–21). They also determined jurisdictional matters (21:2). There was a chief judge at the regional shrine along with a presiding priest (Levite). They represented a supreme court to which cases that could not be solved at the local level were sent. It is not clear how their realms of authority were determined but, presumably, the Levite ruled in cultic matters and the chief judge ruled in civil matters. That these two regions of authority were separate is prescient. It illustrates some measure of distinction between church and state. At the same time, all of the law, both cultic and civil, was considered to have come from Yahweh, and all of it demanded compliance.

This law is presented as if it were given *de novo* to Israel east of the Jordan River before entering the land of Canaan. That picture is story, not history. Law emerges from human experience and the Code of Deuteronomy is no different in this respect. As has been noted, about half of it shares common ground with the Covenant Code in

Exodus 20:22–23:19, acknowledged as early law. There is a comment against moving a property marker, which suggests that Israel had long been in the land at the time that the law was enacted. "You must not move your neighbor's boundary marker, *set up by former generations,* on the property that will be allotted to you in the land that the Lord your God is giving you to possess" (19:14). If the former generations were Canaanites, it wouldn't matter. The latter part of this law seems to have been added to reflect Mosaic authorship.

Much of the law reads as if it is active in the present. For example, the case of a dead body being found near the border of two townships could only derive from real life situations (21:1–9). And the offering of the first fruits assumes a well-established practice at a well-established shrine (26:1–11).

It is characteristic for the law to be given a context. We have seen in the previous chapter that the law of Leviticus was preceded in the latter part of Exodus by an extensive description of the Tabernacle, where so much of the levitical law was implemented, a structure so elegant, so filled with the spiritual presence of awe that the most stringent rules had to be imposed for protection from the cleansing power of holiness. Psychologically, this prepares the reader to absorb the statutes in their specifics with the most ardent reverence.

Similarly, the law given at Mt. Sinai, the Ten Commandments and the Covenant Code (Exodus 20:1–23:19), takes place with the people surrounding the mountain, having washed their clothes, awaiting the fierce announcement of the presence of the Lord: the thunder and lightning, the trumpet blast, the quaking of the mountain all wrapped in smoke (Exodus 19). This, also, is intended to prepare the mind and heart of the reader for the awesome gravity of the law.

Likewise, the Code of Deuteronomy (12–26) and its appended old law (27) is given a context. It is different in scope but is no less fraught with fervor. Here, the presence of the Lord pervades the whole community. It is not fearsome, lest the priestly intricacies of cultic propriety be violated, but it is fearsome, lest the Ten Commandments and the Deuteronomic Code be violated: those precepts that define and mold the community of faith in political, social, economic, and religious terms. This context is historical in form though, as stated, not historical in fact. Yahweh led Israel from Mt. Sinai through the wilderness for 40 years, sustaining them, protecting them, correcting them. At times, Yahweh reached the breaking point in tolerating their wayward tendencies.

Moses, the mediator, had to then restrain, as it were, the Lord's destructive intentions, even as, at other times, he appealed to the Lord for guidance out of frustration from the people's antagonism.

In spite of Yahweh's providential care, the wilderness is an unsettling experience. (I have shifted, deliberately, from the past tense to the present because the emphasis in this text is appropriating the past for the present. All that is said about the past in Deuteronomy is communicated by Moses in the present. One could argue that a summary of all of this material should be in the present tense. Moses is speaking to all Israel between the past and the future. The past is made to provide the foundation for the future. The focus points to the land that Yahweh is giving Israel for their possession.) Here, on the eastern bank of the Jordan, Moses gives them the statutes and the ordinances that they are to observe in the occupation of the land. For six chapters before the Code (6–11) and three chapters after it (28–30), with one persuasive argument after another, Moses impresses upon Israel—hence the reader—that living by this law is a life or death decision.

> *I call heaven and earth to witness against you today that I have set before you life and death, blessings and curses. Choose life so that you and your descendants may live, loving the Lord your God, obeying him, and holding fast to him; for that means life to you and length of days, so that you may live in the land that the Lord swore to give to your ancestors, to Abraham, to Isaac, and to Jacob* (30:19–20).

The Lord chooses Israel to be his people, not because of any special merit, but because he loves them (7:7–8).

There was probably a tent. There was probably a mountain associated with the divine presence. There was probably a wilderness journey. But the traditions that developed around them are story, story intended to convey seminal power. That story applies not only to the Israel of the past but to every generation of Israel: In all the law and the preaching about it, God is present. 📖

Notes

1. C. H. J. de Geus, "Judah" in *Anchor Bible Dictionary,* 3:1035.

2. Finkelstein and Silberman, *The Bible Unearthed,* 243.

3. G. von Rad, "Deuteronomy" in *Interpreter's Dictionary of the Bible,* 1:833.

4. Moshe Weinfeld, *Deuteronomy 1–11* (New York: Doubleday, 1991), 13–14.

5. George E. Mendenhall and Gary A Herion, "Covenant" in *Anchor Bible Dictionary,* 1:1180–82.

6. Ibid., 1183.

7. Ibid., 1185.

8. Weinfeld, *Deuteronomy 1–11,* 7.

9. Ibid., 9.

10. Mendenhall and Herion, "Covenant", 1187–88.

11. Weinfeld, *Deuteronomy 1–11,* 17.

12. E. W. Nicholson, *Deuteronomy and Tradition* (Philadelphia: Fortress Press, 1967), 22–36.

13. Gerhard von Rad, *Studies in Deuteronomy* (Chicago: Henry Regnery Co., 1953), 45–59.

14. Ibid., 49.

15. Ibid., 50-51.

16. Niels Peter Lemche, "Israel, History of (Premonarchic Period)" trans. Frederick Cryer in *Anchor Bible Dictionary,* 3:527.

Biblical Or Not?

In chapter one, I noted that all modern translations of the Old Testament into English are based primarily on a single manuscript, the Leningrad Codex, dated 1008 CE. I also noted that this manuscript along with the early 10th-century Aleppo Codex represent the apex of the development of the Masoretic Text, that prodigious effort by the Masoretes from about 500 to 900 to solidify the text for all time. The Jewish canon had been determined in three stages. The Torah or Pentateuch is thought to have been completed in its present form, perhaps by Ezra, in the 5th century BCE. The Prophets are a collection that gradually accumulated into its final form by the 2nd century BCE, possibly earlier. The last stage, in which the remaining books received some stamp of authority, took place around the end of the 1st century CE. Subsequently, the means for securing the text both for meaning and for enunciation was devised.

The Jewish canon is the basis for the Old Testament in Protestant Bibles, but Roman Catholic Bibles include the Apocrypha, which are derived largely from the Septuagint. Some other versions, from early times, include books that belong to the Pseudepigrapha, a large collection of writings from early Judaism. "Some of the 'pseudepigrapha' were valued and used in different Christian communities, and thus came to be preserved (sometimes with Christian interpolations) in Greek, Syriac, Ethiopic, and other versions."[1] To be specific, some Syriac manuscripts include 2 Baruch, 4th Ezra, Odes of Solomon, and Psalms of Solomon. Some Armenian manuscripts include 4th Ezra and the Testaments of the Twelve Patriarchs. Some Ethiopic manuscripts include I Enoch, Jubilees, and the Ascension of Isaiah.[2]

The books of the Apocrypha and Pseudepigrapha bear a close

relationship to Old Testament literature in one of several ways. Some, like the Testaments of the Twelve Patriarchs, expand and amplify the narrative traditions. Some, like the Book of Enoch, build new literary developments around leading legendary figures. Some, like Tobit, are stories that depict models of faith as Jews. Some, like the Wisdom of Solomon, continue creative poetic expression in well-established forms. Some, like the Books of Maccabees, continue the historical traditions. Perhaps one can characterize other relationships but, in general, it can be said that all of these books represent the ongoing literary activity of the Jewish people as a faith community and are historically interconnected. In this literature, the faith and experience of Israel continued to be expressed in traditions common to his past.

The Apocrypha

In the history of the Bible, nothing is so confusing as the identification and position of the Apocrypha, and the confusion is still growing. The meaning of the term, the number of books that are included, which books they are, the names of those books, the measure of authority they bear in relation to the Old and New Testaments, who determines their inclusion or exclusion in printed Bibles, all manifest striking differences in the ongoing tradition of the churches with little expectation of resolution.

The word apocrypha means "hidden things" or "obscure things." Since many Jews believed that the inspired writings were composed between Moses and Ezra, books that came to be called Apocrypha were either ascribed to one of the major biblical figures or were additions to the canonical books. Thus, they were hidden. In the context of Protestant tradition, "Apocrypha" has come to represent 15 books that have circulated with the Bible but are designated noncanonical. These books are:

- ‣ Tobit
- ‣ Judith
- ‣ Additions to the Book of Esther (1)
- ‣ Wisdom of Solomon
- ‣ Ecclesiasticus, or Sirach
- ‣ Baruch
- ‣ Letter of Jeremiah (2)
- ‣ Prayer of Azariah and the Song of the Three Jews (3)

▸   Susanna (3)
▸   Bel and the Dragon (3)
▸   I Maccabees
▸   II Maccabees
▸   I Esdras
▸   II Esdras
▸   Prayer of Manasseh

In Roman Catholic tradition, "apocrypha" refers to the last three of these 15 and includes other outside books known as "pseudepigrapha" in Protestant tradition. Seven others of the 15 are designated "deutero-canonical" in Roman Catholic tradition, meaning that they were declared canonical at a later time. The other five, being continuing traditions of the books of Esther (1), Baruch (2), and Daniel (3), are inserted into or appended to those books.

Orthodox Bibles include all of these books plus a few more in their canon. They do not have a category termed apocrypha, but place one other outside book in an appendix (4 Maccabees).

Early English Bibles included the Apocrypha as a collection placed after the New Testament, but some printings of both the Geneva Bible and the King James Version appeared without them and later, especially from the 19th century on, their omission was standard practice, as noted in the *New Oxford Annotated Bible,* by Bruce Metzger.[3] It is noteworthy, however, that both this study Bible and the Harper Collins Study Bible include all of the books found in Protestant, Roman Catholic, and Orthodox Bibles, following Protestant practice in defining the Old Testament, so that the list of books assigned to the Apocrypha totals 18. It means that in these Bibles, "Apocrypha" has been redefined as the collection of supplementary books that allows each tradition to complete its canon by selection, and otherwise recognize those of secondary standing.

The most confusing aspect of the Apocrypha has to do with the nomenclature associated with the extended Ezra-Nehemiah traditions, which are mostly divided into four parts, the titles of which, I–IV Esdras, are applied differently in different Bibles. Each of the two study Bibles mentioned above has a chart showing the different designations, to the bewilderment of the reader.

In broader perspective, the Apocrypha are an extension of a widespread phenomenon from early Judaism, namely the continuation of written traditions that are in some sense related to those already established, that is, to the Old Testament books. There is a large collection of books related to the Old Testament known as Pseudepigrapha, although the meaning of the term "falsely attributed writings" does not always apply. There are about 65.[4] The Dead Sea Scrolls, also from early Judaism, have the distinction of being a library within an immediate community. They include a few of the Apocrypha and Pseudepigrapha along with the biblical scrolls and represent a wide variety of works that reflect an active communal life, steeped in biblical tradition, that through commentary, rules, and extended psalms interpreted the present and future by the traditions of the past.

Given the large number of books associated with the Old Testament traditions in early Judaism, why did the books of the Apocrypha continue to be passed on in Christian tradition with the biblical books and not others? The answer is that all of them except II Esdras were found in the Bible of the early Christians, the Septuagint, which is the Greek Old Testament, and II Esdras was found in the Old Latin versions, which also circulated in the Western churches. They were a recognized part of the canon, at least through the 4th century, and numerous Church Fathers quoted them as Scripture. At the end of the 4th century, Jerome was commissioned to make a new Latin translation, and he followed the Hebrew, which, of course, does not contain the Apocrypha. Consequently, he assigned them a separate status, but through the ongoing centuries his designation was not always maintained.[5] The Protestant Reformers followed Jerome, but the Roman Catholic Church followed the broader tradition and adopted the Apocrypha as Scripture. The books of the Pseudepigrapha, until recently, remained largely forgotten.

Our present interest in the Apocrypha is not in its thought content per se but as a witness to the development of Old Testament literature. As we have seen, its position is and has been ambiguous. Its recognized authority covers a wide range, from Eastern Orthodoxy, which includes all of these books as Scripture, to Jews and most Protestants, which have excluded them entirely. The root of this ambiguity goes back to the end of the 1st century CE, when the Jews defined their Bible and the Christians followed the Septuagint. While Protestant Bibles and modern Jewish translations enumerate 39 books in the Old Testament, early Jewish tradition assigns 24 to the same materials. Each of the following was considered as one book: I & II Samuel, I & II Kings, I & II Chronicles, Ezra & Nehemiah, and the 12 minor prophets.

This tradition goes back to II Esdras 14:44–48, where Ezra is told to write down 94 books, 24 of which were to be made public. The other 70, whatever they were, were intended for the wise. Josephus enumerates 22, assigning five to Moses, 13 to the prophets, and four as hymns and precepts. All of these were to have been written between the time of Moses and that of Artaxerxes—and Ezra. We do not know what Josephus included in the second and third groups. He notes that Jewish history was written after Artaxerxes but it does not have scriptural authority because the age of prophecy has passed. The sacred books, he says, contain doctrines for which Jews are willing to die. Moreover, he states that nothing has been added to them or taken from them.[6] Josephus wrote this at the end of the 1st century CE, when the rabbis of Palestinian Judaism were finalizing their canon.

The Apocrypha has come to us through Alexandrian Judaism, the home of the Septuagint. It represents the extension of some Old Testament traditions. There are several different forms that this extension takes. In some cases, an apocryphal book serves to expand an Old Testament book and, in the Septuagint, has been prefixed, inserted, or appended to enlarge the scope of the book. This is the case with The Additions to the Book of Esther and The Additions to the Greek Book of Daniel. Perhaps it would be more accurate to say that what in these traditions are called books of the Apocrypha are really extracted portions of the Septuagint version of these Old Testament books so that the latter conform to the Masoretic Text. In the case of Esther, there are six additions labeled A-F that are interspersed into the Greek equivalent of the Hebrew text. Older editions of the Apocrypha in English simply join them together. Recent editions of the Apocrypha, however, reproduce the entire Septuagint version of the Book of Esther in translation.

With the case of the Book of Daniel, there are three additions that are recognized as three different books of the Apocrypha. The first, known as The Prayer of Azariah and the Song of the Three Jews, appears as an insert in the middle of chapter three of the Greek equivalent of the Masoretic Text. The other two, Bel and the Dragon and Susanna, are appended to the end of the Book.

Looking at these Esther and Daniel traditions in their historical context, the Apocrypha presents a misleading picture. In reality, what we have are two editions of the Book of Esther and two editions of the Book of Daniel. Some comparison can be drawn with the two editions of the Book of Jeremiah that I mentioned in the first chapter, except that the "additions" to Esther and Daniel are more clear-cut. Of the Old Testament books, these two are among the latest to have been written and the "additions" are not far behind the original text. The Book of Jeremiah, on the other hand, went through a much longer process of transmission before the movement of text stabilization, and the differences between the two editions of this book are much more complex.

There are two books of the Apocrypha that belong to the Jeremiah traditions: Baruch and the Letter of Jeremiah. While they are combined in the Vulgate as a single book, they are found in the Septuagint as separate books, the order being: Jeremiah, Baruch, Lamentations, and Letter of Jeremiah. The man Baruch is linked to the man Jeremiah as his amanuensis in the Book of Jeremiah 36 and 45. There is no mention of the authorship of Lamentations in the Hebrew Bible, but the Septuagint assigns it to Jeremiah in an introductory verse. A similar introduction is found in the Letter of Jeremiah. So all of these books belong together as Jeremiah traditions.

In the first chapter, I noted the striking differences between the Septuagint version of the Book of Jeremiah and that of the Masoretic Text. The latter shows extensive expansions in relation to the former so that Emanuel Tov posits two editions. This, in effect, is an example of the growth of tradition. But beyond that, when one examines the Book of Jeremiah on strictly literary grounds, it is so disorganized, so much of a hodge-podge of literary units, large and small, that it can only be recognized as a collection. Robert Carroll, in his recent massive commentary, says of it: "Such a miscellaneous collection of discrete and disparate writings describes well the book of Jeremiah." He then goes on to enumerate about 25 independent units or smaller collections and says, "These many 'books' melded into one large work and held together by a redactional framework explaining the individual parts as the work of Jeremiah constitute the Jeremiah tradition."[7] In a summary statement, he says, "The key to the interpretation of the Book of Jeremiah is the analysis of its redactional history."[8]

The Jeremiah tradition, however, did not end with his book. The Book of Lamentations, assigned to Jeremiah by the Septuagint, is a group of five independent laments over the destruction of Jerusalem in 586 BCE, probably written soon thereafter. Baruch, written much later, is also a collection of several parts, including in some manuscripts the Letter of Jeremiah. Indeed, the Baruch tradition continued into the post-biblical era with three additional books, all probably written in the

2nd century CE, known as 2 Baruch, 3 Baruch, and 4 Baruch.

The Ezra traditions, as noted above, have been the subject of much confusion because of the dual use of the Hebrew and Greek forms of the same name, Ezra and Esdras, and their inconsistent application to the same material. If we adopt the nomenclature of Protestant tradition, some clarity can be gained by recognizing that I Esdras is mostly biblical material and II Esdras is post-biblical literature. It is difficult to know why the Septuagint included I Esdras since most of it is a duplication of material found in the biblical books. There is just one section of material not found elsewhere, chapters 3:1–5:6, known as the Tale of the Three Guardsmen. The rest of the book includes the basic content of II Chronicles 35–36, the whole of Ezra, and Nehemiah 7:6–8:12.

I Esdras does not mention Nehemiah. It is the Ezra story. According to Bruce Metzger, it is not a translation of the canonical material but both Ezra-Nehemiah and I Esdras used the same sources.[9] The two really belong side by side as witnesses to a disorderly Ezra and Nehemiah tradition. But I Esdras was not a part of the Masoretic textual tradition, so it was not eligible for canonical status either in the Jewish or Protestant communities.

Ezra and Nehemiah represent the historical genre. When placed under the scrutiny of the historical time line, however, they consist of sections of material that do not follow an orderly process. Attempts to rearrange these sections leave much to be desired. Apparently, Ezra-Nehemiah was not written as an integrated history but as a collection of sources describing a variety of events in the resettlement of Jerusalem after the Babylonian Exile covering a period of 100 to 150 years.

There is some relationship between Chronicles and the Ezra-Nehemiah traditions. The last paragraph of II Chronicles is repeated at the beginning of the Book of Ezra and, as we have seen, I Esdras links the last two chapters of II Chronicles to the Book of Ezra. Whether or not these belong together in their historical development is at present unknown.

II Esdras represents the end of the Ezra tradition, written during the early Christian centuries, probably under both Jewish and Christian authorship. Ezra is an elevated seer in dialogue with an angel about God's justice, considering Israel's condition amid the evil of other nations. Ezra sees visions, reminiscent of Daniel, about the last things. In the last of seven visions, he is given a divine potion by which he dictates the revelation that has been lost: the 24 books of the Old Testament plus 70 others intended only for the wise men of Israel. The figure of Ezra as the extraordinary holy man and scribe of I Esdras and Ezra-Nehemiah has been elevated to the heavenly realm with superhuman powers of vision, understanding, and memory.

In terms of understanding these books at face value, it makes more sense to group them together as the Ezra traditions rather than dividing between the canonical Ezra-Nehemiah and the apocryphal I & II Esdras. Not that we have a coherent story of Ezra but, rather, an example of a tradition and the forms that it took.

The Prayer of Manasseh is an addition to the tradition about King Manasseh of Judah in the Second Book of Chronicles. As will be seen, the Books of Chronicles utilize considerable source material from the Books of Kings but frequently modify it. In Kings, Manasseh is considered the worst king in Judah's history. The extent of his evil, alone, provides the reason for the destruction of Jerusalem and the rejection of Israel by the Lord (II Kings 21:10–15). And there is no amelioration. Chronicles omits these severe consequences. In their place, Manasseh is said to have been taken captive to Babylon where he uttered a prayer of repentance and was restored by God to his kingship in Jerusalem, after which he reformed his ways. Later tradition supplied this Prayer of Manasseh. Here is an example of how tradition evolves and is sometimes transformed. The Prayer of Manasseh would have been unthinkable to the editor of the Second Book of Kings.

While the Books of Tobit and Judith do not continue thematic traditions of the Old Testament, they do extend the literary tradition of the novelette exemplified by the Books of Ruth and Esther. All of these books feature a model of Israelite devotion who, in spite of adversity, becomes an agent of redemption. Although Ruth is not an Israelite, she becomes one by choice, and her exceptional self-sacrifice provides an ideal image for an ordinary woman or one of deprived circumstances. Tobit epitomizes the common man of consummate piety, observing the law strictly and doing deeds of charity. Esther and Judith are noble women of great courage who risk their lives in times of severe crises, using their womanly ways: Judith to save the Temple and Jerusalem from the advancing Assyrian army, and Esther to save her people from the threat of annihilation. Judith and Esther were closely associated by the early Church Fathers, several of whom, through the 4th century, rejected Esther as canonical. The same debate about Esther's canonicity was found among the rabbis during the first two or three centuries. The book, itself, is virtually devoid of religious elements, and even though the story serves to explain the reason for the festival of Purim, that festival is not Mosaic, a status that many Jews required. Of all the canonical books, Esther, alone, is absent from the Dead Sea Scrolls.[10] However, the canonical status of Ruth was never in doubt.

The Wisdom of Solomon and Sirach, known also as Ecclesiasticus, are extensions of the wisdom literature of the Old Testament, especially of the Book of Proverbs. Wisdom—the short title for Wisdom of Solomon—and much of Sirach utilize the instruction genre common to Proverbs 1–9. Sometimes hortatory, sometimes in the form of prayer, sometimes interpretations of Israel's history, sometimes simply descriptive of wisdom, there is an evaluation of human actions, deeds, and motivations in relation to wisdom as divine revelation. The much longer Sirach also uses the wisdom sentence, common to Proverbs 10:1–22:16, but usually in extended groupings on a common subject.

Examined intrinsically, these three books are similar in content, reflecting the same perspective on wisdom, faith, and experience. Deservedly, they occupied the same ground in Alexandrian Judaism and so, also, in the Roman Catholic canon. Rabbinic Judaism included only Proverbs as did the Protestant canon, following Luther, but Sirach was considered scripture among some Jews as late as the 2nd century.[11]

I and II Maccabees continue the tradition of historical writing in ancient Israel. They record the crisis in the 2nd century BCE in which the Jews, faithful to the law, were subject to the most severe persecution at the hands of the Syrian rulers, and the successful revolt by the Maccabeans in defeating them. II Maccabees records a more vivid and fanciful account of the divine forces that supported the faithful. I Maccabees, in its prosaic manner, sets forth the background of the crisis, which is so essential for understanding the Book of Daniel. Bruce Metzger, following Luther, deems it worthy of the status of scripture. He writes:

> *It must be admitted that, from one point of view,it is some-*
> *what strange that so Jewish a book a I Maccabees was not*
> *accepted by the Rabbis as part of the Scriptures, and that*
> *the Hebrew original was allowed to disappear.*[12]

He quotes Luther's similar sentiment:

> *This is another of those books not included in the Hebrew*
> *Scriptures, although in its style, in language and words, it*

closely resembles the rest of the books of Holy Scripture, and would not have been unworthy to be reckoned among them, because it is a very necessary and useful book for the understanding of the eleventh chapter of the prophet Daniel.[13]

According to Jonathan Goldstein, I Maccabees was rejected from the canon because the author claimed that "God had chosen Mattathias' line to be both high priests and kings," which later history disproved, and because he denied belief in the resurrection.[14]

The Books of Maccabees are found in two of the three earliest and most important manuscripts of the Septuagint. Considering the Septuagint manuscripts as a whole, it is notable that while the Pentateuch always comes first followed by the historical books, including Ruth and Chronicles, which the Hebrew Bible assigns to the Writings, there is no established order for the remaining books except that the Prophets are grouped together. Maccabees is usually grouped with Esther, Tobit, Judith, and Esdras 1 and 2. Of this group, Esther and Ezra-Nehemiah (2 Esdras in the Septuagint) became part of the Hebrew canon, later adopted by Protestants, while the others found their way into the Protestant Apocrypha. The Dead Sea Scrolls include three fragments of Ezra (not including Nehemiah) but no portion of Esther.

The Pseudepigrapha

The word pseudepigrapha is probably unknown to most people. It means "falsely attributed writings." Its usage in church history goes back to the early Christian centuries when it referred to writings about or by leading biblical characters, such as Abraham, Moses, and Elijah. In recent times, it has become a broader category, referring to a collection of writings spanning the period 250 BCE–200 CE that enlarge on Old Testament traditions. They are of Jewish origin but some of them reflect Christian interpolation, editing, or rewriting.[15] "Many of the writings in it were, of course, as influential in Jewish circles (especially before the end of the Bar Kokhba revolt in 135 CE) and in Christian circles (especially before the Council of Nicea in 325 CE) as the writings later canonized."[16]

These writings dropped out of circulation in both Jewish and Christian communities. In 1913 R.H. Charles published a massive two-volume work, *The Apocrypha and Pseudepigrapha of the Old Testament in English,* which was the only substantial source available until James Charlesworth edited the most comprehensive collection yet, *The Old Testament Pseudepigrapha,* also a large two-volume work published in 1985. It is in the Charlesworth collection that I find, for this study, the ongoing traditions related to the Old Testament narratives and poetry.

Obviously, we cannot discuss all of the Pseudepigrapha here. Our purpose is to show how Old Testament traditions continued to be creatively developed in the ongoing history of Israel. Given the enormity of the Pseudepigrapha and the limitations demanded by our study, we can select only a few for illustration. I have chosen the major examples of the Genesis traditions as they are represented in the Pseudepigrapha. They are:

1. Jubilees
2. Life of Adam and Eve
3. Apocalypse of Abraham
4. Testaments of the Twelve Patriarchs
5. Joseph and Asenath

While the Enoch traditions represent the most extensive treatment of any figure in the Pseudepigrapha, and may be the most important for understanding early Judaism and early Christianity, so little is said about Enoch in the Genesis narrative that the Book of Enoch can be considered an entirely new development. Enoch uniquely provides the clues for two of the most important subjects of early Judaism: the heavenly world and the solar year. As the sole antediluvian patriarch who did not die but was transported directly to heaven (Genesis 5:24), he was the suitable agent to describe "the secrets of the mysteries of the universe, the future of the world, and the predetermined course of human history."[17]

Apart from his position in the genealogy, the only other reference in Genesis to his life is that he lived 365 years (Genesis 5:23). The Enoch traditions make much of the solar year, which, of course, is associated with the number of his years. It must be recognized that, although the themes of the fallen angels (Genesis 6:1–4) and the great Flood are prominent in I Enoch, they reflect such a small portion of Genesis that I hesitate to think of the Enoch traditions as representing an extension of the Genesis traditions. Enoch should be seen as a separate development. It is worthy of note that Enoch is the only book of the Pseudepigrapha that is quoted in the New Testament (Jude verse 14).

The Genesis Traditions
in the Pseudepigrapha

1. Jubilees–2nd century BCE

Jubilees is a version of the Book of Genesis, sometimes expanded and sometimes abbreviated, with a few selected portions of the Book of Exodus. In the introductory chapter, the Lord commands an angel to write for Moses the whole history of Israel including the future, from the creation to the consummation, when the eternal temple will be established in Jerusalem forever and the Lord will dwell with his people. The angel, in turn, instructs Moses to write the history from creation up to the present moment, that is, his presence on Mt. Sinai. This includes the angel's telling Moses about his birth and, as if he didn't know it, about his flight into the wilderness, the plagues—though abbreviated—and Israel's escape from Egypt. In keeping with Jubilees' cultic emphasis, the Passover, in a lengthy treatment, is given the most prominent place.

The whole account of this history from creation on, which Moses writes, is divided into the time frame of 49 jubilees plus 9 years with the expectation of 40 years to the event of the entrance into Canaan. A jubilee is the 50th year, as denoted in Leviticus 25, its definitive treatment. It is a year of release, when the land reverts to its original owners and all bonded people are freed. In the Book of Jubilees, Israel is to enter the land of Canaan in the 50th year of the 50th jubilee, a jubilee of jubilees. The land is theirs and the people are free. Thus the name of the book, "Jubilees."

Part of the expansion of the Genesis traditions and those of the early chapters of Exodus is the inclusion of legal material from the latter part of Exodus, from Leviticus and Numbers. One finds much adornment of the biblical material. For example, when Abram moves from Ur to Canaan, the Angel of the Presence teaches him Hebrew. The wives of the antediluvian Patriarchs are named. There is explanation of the additional day needed to complete the 365-day year, so central to the structure of the book.

On the other hand, some traditions have been shortened. The account of the plagues has been reduced to little more than the mention of what they were. The story of the Flood has been condensed considerably. The Joseph stories have been abbreviated. The descendants of

Esau are limited to a small portion of the narrative given in Genesis 36. As will be noted, Jacob's blessing of Ephraim and Manasseh is transferred to two other tribes.

Jubilees is an excellent example of the rewriting of tradition in which the priorities of the community at the time of the writing are revealed. As Wintermute writes, "Like most writers of history, the author of Jubilees was concerned to review critical events of the past in order to expose their significance for understanding his own contemporary political, social, or cultural situation."[18] Moses, the most important cult figure of post-exilic Judaism, is the agent of revelation, having been granted the vision of Israel's history to its completion. The Sabbath serves as an envelope figure for that whole history, given emphatic treatment both at the apex of creation and at the very end of the history that Moses is told to write. And the ordinances of the cultic life, which achieved their fruition in the flowering of Judaism, are superimposed here and there on that earlier history, for they were seen as the means of purifying Israel.

Some examples of the intrusion of cultic law into the early traditions illustrate the usage. After Eve's creation, when she is brought into the Garden of Eden, the laws of purification after childbirth from Leviticus 12 are given, even before the Fall. When Noah is allowed to eat meat after the Flood but is forbidden the blood (Genesis 9:4), Jubilees injects the laws of Leviticus 17:10–12. This is followed by an elaborate treatment of the Feast of Weeks, a law derived from Exodus 23:16 and 34:22. Further, when Noah plants a vineyard and makes wine (Genesis 9:20–21), Jubilees has him preparing a feast with the detailed prescriptions for sacrifice following the patterns of Numbers 28–29. Finally, in this anachronistic treatment of cultic law, Noah teaches his sons and grandsons the law of the first fruits based on Leviticus 19:23–25 and 25:2–7.

Jubilees provides a second curse on Canaan, the son of Ham. In a story that has no basis in the biblical literature, Canaan is said to occupy land assigned to Shem and is warned of the curse by Ham and his other sons.

The story of Abraham also includes major expansions of cultic prescriptions. In Genesis, circumcision is first instituted with Abraham. While it is given there as a sign of the covenant for all generations (Genesis 17:9–14, 23–27), Jubilees imputes it to the angels, makes it the basis for Israel's election—in opposition to Ishmael and Esau—and foresees Israel's rejection of this most compelling ordinance. On this last point, the appeal of Greek culture under the Seleucids seems clearly to be indicated (II Maccabees 4:11–17; I Maccabees 1:11–15).

Not only does Jubilees have Isaac born on the Feast of First Fruits but, in a lengthy narrative, Abraham observes the Feast of Booths according to patterns found in Leviticus 23:33–40 and Numbers 29:12–38. Lengthy additions to the biblical narrative are assigned to Abraham's final days. His farewell testimony to Isaac is replete with numerous particulars for proper sacrifice, largely from Leviticus. Then he celebrates the Feast of First Fruits, a commemorative meal with his family. Finally, he bestows a blessing on Jacob, after which they both lie down in the same bed and Abraham blesses him again. Indeed, there is no end to the blessings that Jacob receives. Rebecca bestows a blessing. The biblical blessing from Isaac by mistake is reproduced in full. Finally, Isaac provides a joint blessing for Jacob and Esau. In later narratives, there is war between Jacob and Esau. Perhaps reflecting the enormous enmity against the Edomites after the destruction of Jerusalem in 586 BCE, Jacob kills Esau.

I have stated that Jacob's blessing of Ephraim and Manasseh is omitted in Jubilees. The pattern of that story, however, is represented in Isaac's blessing Jacob's sons, Levi and Judah. Of course, these are the two important tribes in post-exilic Judaism. Levi is the priesthood and Judah is Israel.

In Genesis, Jacob has two profound experiences at Bethel (28:10–22, 35:9–15). In Jubilees, he plans to build there but in a vision, the Lord tells him not to build a sanctuary there because "this is not the place" (32:23). Obviously, as the term in Deuteronomy had come to be identified, "the place" is Jerusalem. Since the tribes of the North had long since disappeared when Jubilees was written, the focus was on the people and places that maintained their importance.

The Joseph stories, somewhat abbreviated, are reproduced in Jubilees. The end of the story, however, has a curious twist. In Genesis, Joseph asks that his bones be carried from Egypt to the land of Canaan, and later tradition says that they were (Exodus 13:19; Joshua 24:32). Nothing is said about the bones of his brothers. Jubilees states that "the bones of the children of Jacob, all except the bones of Joseph" (46:9) were buried in the patriarchal tomb, the cave of Machpelah. But nothing is said here of Joseph's bones. This is another example of transferring the priority to the tradition that is current. Joseph represents the extinct Northern Kingdom.

The rationale for the Book of Jubilees is presented as revealing to Moses the history of Israel from Creation to the time of his adulthood, after which he would know it himself. This allows for the established doctrine that Moses wrote the whole Torah, except for the account of his death. The inclusion of the early chapters of Exodus leading up to his presence on Mt. Sinai not only fulfills this function but provides for the lengthy treatment of Passover that, with the similar emphasis on the Sabbath that ends the book, are the most imposing cultic observances. Cultic observances defined the life of Judaism when Jubilees was written and rewriting Genesis and early Exodus was a means of reordering and emphasizing the priorities of the time.

2. Life of Adam and Eve—1st century CE

This is a midrash—an extensive commentary—on the stories of the Garden of Eden and Cain and Abel. There is both a Greek and a Latin version. In general, the content of the two is similar, but in exposition and arrangement, the differences are substantial so that they need to be seen as separate treatments of a common tradition. There are numerous manuscripts in both languages dating from the middle to late Middle Ages. Johnson believes it was composed in Hebrew during the 1st century CE.[19] It appears, then, that we are witnessing the effects of tradition in two different senses. First, when it was written, the elaborate treatment of the ancient story allows the intrusion of beliefs and concepts current at the time of the writing. Paradise is a totally different place from Earth. There is no hunger; the food of angels is always present. There is no guilt. There is no pain. In the second sense, the differences between the Latin and Greek versions must be seen in the transmission of these two traditions independently.

The Latin version opens with Adam and Eve struggling to find food after having been driven out of Paradise. They find only food for animals. Conscious of their sin, they decide to demonstrate their penitence emphatically. Adam tells Eve to go to the Tigris River and stand in water up to her neck for 37 days. He, likewise, will stand up to his neck in the Jordan River for 40 days. After 18 days, Satan approaches Eve and deceives her a second time, telling her that God has accepted her repentance and has sent him to bring her to the place where the food of Paradise is to be found. She follows him while he leads her to Adam. When Adam sees Eve and the devil together, he is infuriated. He chastises Eve for breaking the penance. She, in turn, rebukes the devil, who complains that he was cast out from the presence of God because he refused to worship the image of God in Adam. After Adam prays to God to remove the devil, which He does, Adam completes the 40 days of repentance.

The Greek version begins with the story of Cain and Abel. It is a brief account compared to its parallel in the Latin version. In the latter, Eve accepts full responsibility for the Fall and journeys lamentably toward the West expecting to die. But she is found to be pregnant, and when her birth pangs begin, she cries out for Adam, who is far away. As a miniature love story would have it, Adam hears her cry intuitively and hastens to her side. There, he prays for Eve, and the Lord sends Michael and a dozen angels, who minister to her. Cain is born and, subsequently, Abel. Eve has a dream of Cain killing Abel, after which it really happens. During Adam's remaining 800 years, Seth is born as well as 30 sons and 30 daughters who people the nations.

The Greek version lacks the descriptive material surrounding Cain's birth, but Eve's dream about his murder of Abel and mention of the other children are given. In this terse account, the one addition to the biblical story is that Cain is excoriated as a son of wrath.

The Latin version continues with Adam's being transported to Paradise by a fiery chariot similar to that which carried Elijah (II Kings 2:11). There, in the presence of God, he is told of his mortality because he disobeyed by listening to Eve. After pleading for the endurance of his spirit, he is told that his seed will continue forever. Then, after expressing utmost heartfelt adoration, he is ushered across the frozen waters surrounding Paradise back to Earth by Michael.

At this point, both versions take on the character of a testament. Adam knows that he is about to die and calls all of his sons to his side to hear his last words. Complaining of his pains, he tells the story of the Fall, which, as he explains, was the source of all his pain. Because of his disobedience, God has told him that his body will be subject to 70 plagues.

There is one hope. In Paradise is a tree of mercy out of which flows oil for assuaging pain. Adam sends Eve and Seth to the gates of Paradise for the oil. On the way, the serpent attacks and bites Seth. Eve takes the responsibility. In fact, throughout the whole work, Eve continually repents for the disobedience in the Garden and is also blamed by Adam for it. Eve condemns the serpent for attacking the image of God but he, in turn, condemns her for eating the forbidden fruit. Seth steps in and vanquishes the beast. As they journey on, Michael, the archangel, meets them and tells them to give up the quest for the oil of mercy because Adam will soon die and the oil will be available only in the last days when all flesh will be resurrected.

In the Greek version, Eve tells the story of the Fall. Here, the devil is a wandering spirit who speaks through the mouth of the serpent. He also takes the form of an angel and worships God with the other angels—the ultimate deceiver. Eve confesses that the serpent allured her by praising the glory of the plant and enticed her by claiming omniscient effects from eating its fruit. He led her to the tree and poisoned its fruit, after which she ate, and having so promised the serpent, gave some to Adam. The poison is identified as covetousness, "for covetousness is the origin of every sin" (19:3).

The story continues at length as an elaboration of the Genesis account. The devil speaks through Eve. Michael sounds the trumpet to announce the judgment. The angels cast them out of Paradise. Adam and Eve devoutly repent. Adam asks to eat from the tree of life and is told that this will be allowed only at the time of the resurrection and only if he has kept himself from all evil.

Adam tells Eve of his imminent death and she, in great remorse, confesses the full measure of her sin. An angel lifts her up in time to see a chariot drawn by four eagles bearing Adam heavenward. The Lord, himself, hands him over to Michael who transports him to the third heaven in Paradise. The bodies of Adam and Abel are then prepared ceremonially and buried in the place from which the original dust was taken. Finally, Eve implores God to be allowed to rejoin Adam in death. As she dies, she looks up and says, "God of all, receive my spirit" (42:8). This prayer is remarkably similar to that of Stephen in Acts 7:59. She is buried in Paradise with Abel.

The particularization of Paradise with its seven heavens and coterie of angels belongs to early Judaism. While the biblical story remains the kernel of the Life of Adam and Eve, the expanding tradition went in the direction of the heavenly world. The earthly world is one of pain, guilt, and death.

3. Apocalypse of Abraham—1st to 2nd centuries CE

The Apocalypse of Abraham extends the tradition of Abraham in two ways: (1) It explains why Abraham left Mesopotamia, and (2) it shows how the covenant made with Abraham would be worked out. Thus the work divides into two parts. In the first part (chapters 1 through 8), Abraham assists his father, Terah, who is a maker of idols. Secretly, however, he tests the idols to see if they have any reality. He concludes that his father is the god of the idols. By accident, a wooden idol becomes fuel for the fire that is cooking a meal, proving that the wood, not the god, is what is useful. Abraham's mind goes through a transition in a search for what is real, considering fire, then water, then the sun, moon, and stars. Finally, he recognizes that only a God who created all these things is real. At this point, in his importunity, God breaks through and speaks to him. God tells Abraham to leave his father's house, which he does, whereupon fire consumes Terah and all that he has.

Apart from God's call to Abraham to leave Ur, none of this is found in the Genesis narrative. There, all that is said of Terah is his position in the family line and his move from Ur to Haran, where he died (11:24–32). Abram's call is terse, yet in those three verses (12:1–3) is encapsulated a whole history of Israel's faith. He is told to leave his father's house and go to an unknown land. God will make of him a great nation, will bless him and those who bless him, and in him "all the families of the earth will be blessed."

While the Genesis narratives characterize Abraham's journey through Canaan under Yahweh's direction, the Apocalypse of Abraham depicts his journey into the seven heavens where, after a long prayer of adulation, he has a vision of Ezekiel's throne-chariot in all its fullness. From this vantage point, he sees the whole of creation: the multitude of angels throughout eight firmaments, the Earth with Leviathan in its sea, the Garden of Eden with Adam and Eve tempted by the demon, Azazel, who rules on Earth and corrupts its inhabitants. Abraham sees the Temple with its altar, intended for true worship as God explains, but the chosen people have been idolatrous like Terah. Then Abraham sees the Temple destroyed by the heathen. After a long period, a man emerges from among the heathen but who belongs to Abraham's seed. He is worshiped by some of them but spurned by others and by some of his people. While he has been identified both with Jesus and the Roman emperor, there are difficulties with both assumptions.[20]

Abraham now returns to Earth, and in his bewilderment, he is told to expect a series of 10 plagues against the heathen, after which God will send his chosen one, who will gather his people and inaugurate the final judgment. The wicked will be sent to perdition and the righteous will rejoice. One wonders if Luke's parable of the rich man and Lazarus (16:19–31) assumes the Apocalypse of Abraham as background material or, possibly, Matthew's parable of the Last Judgment (Matthew 25:31–46).

Here and there in the Apocalypse, some descriptive material from the Genesis narratives is included. In the five chapters leading up to Abraham's being borne to the upper regions on the wings of a pigeon, the features of the picturesque sacrifice associated with Yahweh's covenant with Abraham in Genesis 15 are incorporated into the story. In fact, it is described in detail twice (Apocalypse of Abraham 9:4–5; 12:6–8). Also, Yahweh's question to Abraham to look to the stars to see if he can count them (Genesis 15:5) is repeated in Apocalypse 20:3 and the same answer is given (20:5).

Less prominent but noticeable are allusions to the story of the Binding of Isaac (Genesis 22). Abraham is to sacrifice "in the place which I will show you on a high mountain (Apocalypse of Abraham 9:8; cf. Genesis 22:2). He and the angel, Michael, journey to the place of sacrifice, "and we went, the two of us alone together . . ." (Apocalypse of Abraham 12:1; cf. Genesis 22:6, 8). At the place, Abraham complains that he has no sacrifice, but looking around he finds that the sacrificial animals are all there (Apocalypse 12:4–6). This alludes to Isaac's question (22:7) and the ram caught in the thicket (22:13). Another peculiar feature of Genesis 22 found in the Apocalypse is Abraham's being addressed directly by name and his reply, "Here I am." This happens three times in the Genesis narrative. The same is found in the Apocalypse five times.

The Apocalypse of Abraham incorporates enough of the Genesis narratives to root it in the earlier tradition, but the description of the heavenly regions is characteristic of the focus of early Judaism. Here is tradition extending its wings.

4. Testaments of the Twelve Patriarchs, 2nd century BCE

The Testaments of the Twelve Patriarchs is an extension of the traditions about the 12 sons of Jacob. It assumes on the reader's part a knowledge of the Genesis narratives.

A link may be seen with Genesis 49, commonly called the Blessing of Jacob, but should be named, more appropriately, the Testament of

Jacob. In this ancient poem, Jacob is said to project the future condition of the tribes, although in a few cases, only a brief description is given.

The Testaments follow the pattern of each of Jacob's sons, at the end of his life, instructing his children on how to live, often confessing his own faults and warning against particular allurements. Several of them recount their involvement in selling Joseph and deceiving their father. Several also pay homage to Levi and Judah for their paramount roles in Israel's history: Levi and his progeny as the Lord's priests and Judah from whom comes the kingship and messiah. Understandably, the longest accounts are accorded Levi, Judah, and Joseph.

Levi describes his investiture as priest in a dream. God, sitting on His throne in heaven, pronounces the blessing of the priesthood on Levi until He comes to dwell in the midst of Israel. Levi's pre-eminent position is indicated by the dream's portrayal of the archangels in the highest heaven offering sacrifices to the Lord. Yet, after Levi's lofty positioning, where he is anointed with oil and commissioned with all priestly refinement, he foresees the corruption of his offspring leading to the destruction of the sanctuary. All manner of greedy and immoral acts are attributed to them, including the persecution of Jesus, showing Christian modification of an otherwise Jewish text.

Judah describes his enormous prowess in besting both wild animals and warriors, boasting at length of victorious exploits against great odds. Nothing of this character portrait is found in the Genesis narratives except for his brief comparison to a lion in the Blessing of Jacob (49:9). Perhaps it is intended to fortify the image of the tribe of Judah as the first appointed tribe in conquering a substantial portion of the land of Canaan according to Judges 1.

Judah confesses his sexual encounters with two Canaanite women and with Tamar, whom he identifies as Mesopotamian. While recounting the story as told in Genesis 38, he claims that he was drunk in giving vent to his passion. Thus, he warns his children against the sins of promiscuity and drunkenness. This has no linkage to the early narratives. Nor does his railing against the love of money, going so far as to say that it, along with enticement to women, will doom his tribe. Strangely, while Judah acknowledges that God gave him the kingship, he downplays it in two respects. He tells his children that the priesthood is superior, and he predicts that they will become so corrupt that the Lord will bring upon them the most severe punishment. When they repent, however, a messianic figure will emerge to redeem them.

Joseph's story is devoted almost entirely to his ordeal in Egypt while a slave in the house of Potiphar, called Pentephris in the Testaments under the influence of the Septuagint rendering, Petephres. He relates at great length the Memphian woman, as he calls her, trying to entice him to have sexual relations and his repeated rejection of her advances. Thus, he counsels his children to pursue self-control through patience, prayer, and fasting. Finally, he relates a dream in which he sees 12 stags, nine of which are scattered and three of which become lambs. The latter are probably the tribes of Judah, Levi, and Benjamin, which survived. Then, he sees a virgin who gave birth to a spotless lamb, who is identified so distinctly in New Testament imagery that it must represent a Christian interpolation.

In the Testament's precursor, Genesis 49, the blessings of Jacob, Judah, and Joseph stand out as the most important figures, probably reflecting their dominance as tribes in the early period of the monarchy. The monarchy is assigned to Judah and multiple blessings are heaped upon Joseph by the God of Jacob. Levi, however, has no priestly role. He is pictured as a man of violence who is scattered in Israel. The Levites early on were members of other tribes who took on priestly vocations (Judges 17:7–13). Perhaps Genesis 49 antedates that development.

The Testaments reorder the priorities of the tribal figures. Nearly all of the patriarchs counsel their sons to give the highest allegiance to Levi because he represents the priesthood. This includes Judah, whose kingship vies with the sacerdotal but who yields to the higher order. Tradition reflects the changing values of history.

5. Joseph and Aseneth, lst century BCE to 2nd century CE

In the Genesis story of Joseph, Asenath, the daughter of Potiphera, the priest of On, is given to him for a wife by Pharaoh (Genesis 41:45). By her, he begat two sons, Ephraim and Manasseh, the two most important tribes of the Northern Kingdom. This posed a problem in later Israel because in post-exilic Judaism, purity of the family line was most important for one's standing in the community (Ezra 2:59–63). Joseph's marriage, therefore, was nothing short of an embarrassment, and the story of Joseph and Aseneth serves to ameliorate that relationship.

C. Burchard identifies this story as a romance.[21] The emphasis of the story, however, is on the conversion of Aseneth from worship of the idols of Egypt to an undivided devotion to the God whom Joseph worships. To be sure, she is presented as a virgin of impeccable beauty and taste, opulent in finery and resistant to all overtures from men, even Pharaoh's son. She is also offended at her parent's suggestion that she marry Joseph, until she meets him and is overcome by his handsomeness and gentility. But it is her lengthy confessions accompanied by her change of heart in commitment to God and to Joseph that gives her credibility as an ancestress of Israel. And her acceptance as such by a heavenly man who blesses her and intercedes with Joseph to marry her gives her legitimacy that tradition could no longer deny.

In what is, perhaps, a throwback to the Exodus—from the vantage point of the writer—Pharaoh's first-born son plans to kill Joseph and Pharaoh, and take Aseneth for his own wife. He even enlists the tribal brothers who are the sons of Bilhah and Zilpah, Leah's and Rachel's maids, whose legitimacy from the point of view of post-exilic genealogical reckoning was suspect. But the plot fails because Rachel's son, Benjamin, and the sons of Leah prevail. Propriety wins out. Subsequently, Aseneth intercedes for the apostate brothers in a manner that is reflective of Joseph forgiving his brothers at the end of the Genesis story (50:15–21).

Joseph and Aseneth is an example of the continuation of tradition. It is a supplement to the Genesis story, and what it adds enhances the credibility of the earlier tradition in terms of the theological interests prominent at the time of the supplemental writing. Aseneth, because of her character and conversion, is given the stamp of heavenly approval in spite of the fact that she is a non-Israelite. And the romance makes it attractive reading. Tradition that is meaningful is often revised to make it more consistent with the experience of the present community. History and tradition serve the present.

Conclusion

I have entitled this chapter: Biblical Or Not? I have noted that the books of the Apocrypha were biblical for the early churches. They have remained a part of the Bible for the Eastern Churches, which have even included some of the Pseudepigrapha. In the West, through the Middle Ages, they held an ambiguous position. Jerome, in his classic translation, on commission from the Pope, separated them from the books of the Hebrew Bible, giving them a lesser status. However, they continued to circulate among the churches and at the Council of Trent, they were declared a part of the canon.

Luther, like Jerome, separated the books and portions of the Apocrypha from what he found in the Hebrew Bible, placing them at the end of the Old Testament. He declared them noncanonical but worthy to be read. Early English translations followed Luther in this respect. However, reaction against the Apocrypha, especially by Calvinist churches, led to their omission from printed Bibles. The Westminster Confession considered them of no more value than other human writings.[22] Only the Anglican churches have given them an in-between position, using them for worship and moral enrichment but not for doctrine.

The fact that nearly all the Apocrypha belong to the Septuagint indicates that tradition remained a living process in the Jewish community of Alexandria or the Jewish communities of the Mediterranean world. Yet the leaders of Palestinian Judaism moved to draw a sharp distinction between traditions that were inspired from those that were not. In this respect, they were following a process that had begun centuries before when the five books of Moses were recognized as a fixed and final entity termed the Law, probably by Ezra. Subsequently, the Prophets, former and latter, assumed a literary unit when the age of prophecy was seen as complete, perhaps during the 2nd century BCE.

It was the definition of the Writings that occupied the rabbis after the fall of Jerusalem in 70 CE. Whether at the Council of Jamnia in 90 CE or sometime later, decisions were made by the early part of the 2nd century regarding the completion of the Hebrew Bible. To secure their canon, the Jews rejected the Septuagint, conceding it to the Christians, who had adopted it as their Bible. Three new Jewish translations appeared by Aquila, Symmachus, and Theodotion, the version of Aquila being especially valued because it was a near-literal translation of the Hebrew. From then on, the focus was on the vocalization of the text and instituting measures, such as counting the words, to see that it was transmitted precisely. This became the task of the Masoretes. It was completed by the end of the first millennium.

It is only in our time that the Pseudepigrapha are receiving widespread consideration. They are rooted in biblical traditions. The examples that I have used are revisions of Genesis narratives. Two major interests of the religious mentality of early Judaism are reflected in these revisions: (1) the heavenly world, the world of angels and

Paradise where decisions are made about life, death, and history, and (2) the Law, cultic and moral, which both defines Jewish life and separates Jews from others.

Jubilees encompasses the whole of Genesis and the early chapters of Exodus in order to represent it as a revelation from Mt. Sinai. Aided by an angel, Moses writes the history within a division of 50 Jubilees, with emphasis on cultic observances, festivals, circumcision, and, especially, the Sabbath and Passover. The Life of Adam and Eve contrasts Paradise with this world, a life of guilt, pain, and hunger. Paradise is granted to these forebears only in death, but there is hope for the resurrection. In the first part of the Apocalypse of Abraham, the heathen world of Mesopotamia out of which he comes is rejected emphatically by his identification of idolatry and its annihilation. The second part positions Abraham in the seven heavens, where he observes all the corruption on Earth and the whole of history to the final judgment.

The Testaments of the Twelve Patriarchs is permeated with moral instruction, but it also gives special attention to Judaism's leadership roles, especially the priesthood of Levi. Sacrifices are offered to the Lord even in the highest heaven by the archangels. And Judah advises his children that the kingship, which is given to him but will be desecrated by his heirs, is subject to the priesthood. Joseph and Aseneth seems to have the singular purpose of justifying Joseph's marriage to the Egyptian Aseneth following her complete renunciation of idolatry and her conversion to Judaism.

Thus, in these revisions and supplements to the Genesis narratives, a picture of the faith and life of early Judaism is portrayed. The moral law, the cultic law, and the expansive heavenly world—the eventual permanent residence of the faithful—constitute the theological framework for the community of Israel. 📖

1. G. W. Andersen, "Canonical and Non-Canonical" in *The Cambridge History of the Bible,* ed. P. R. Ackroyd and C. F. Evans (Cambridge: Cambridge University Press, 1970), 1:117.

2. S. P. Brock, Joseph M. Alexanian and Rochus Zuurmond, "Versions, Ancient" in *Anchor Bible Dictionary,* 6:795, 806, 808.

3. "The Apocryphal/Deuterocanonical Books of the Old Testament," viii.

4. James H. Charlesworth, "Pseudepigrapha, OT" in Anchor Bible Dictionary, 5:538.

5. Metzger, "The Apocryphal/Deuterocanonical Books of the Old Testament," in *New Oxford Annotated Bible,* iv.

6. Flavius Josephus, "Against Apion," 1:8 in *The Complete Works of Flavius Josephus,* ed. William Whiston (Philadelphia: John E. Potter & Co., n.d.), 710.

7. Robert P. Carroll, Jeremiah (Philadelphia: Westminster Press, 1986), 38.

8. Ibid., 50.

9. Bruce Metzger, *An Introduction to the Apocrypha* (New York: Oxford University Press, 1957), 12.

10. Cary A Moore, *Esther* (Garden City: Doubleday, 1971), xxi–xxix.

11. N. M. Sarna, "Hebrew Bible" in *Encyclopedia Judaica* (Jerusalem: Macmillan, 1971), 4:826.

12. Metzger, *Introduction to the Apocrypha,* 136.

13. Ibid., 136.

14. Jonathan A. Goldstein, *I Maccabees* (Garden City: Doubleday, 1976), 26.

15. James H. Charlesworth, "Pseudepigrapha, OT," 537.

16. Ibid., 539.

17. E. Isaac, "Enoch" in *Old Testament Pseudepigrapha,* ed. James H. Charlesworth (Garden City: Doubleday, 1983), 1:5.

18. O. S. Wintermute, "Jubilees" in *Old Testament Pseudepigrapha,* ed. James H. Charlesworth, 2:37.

19. M. D. Johnson, "Life of Adam and Eve" in *Old Testament Pseudepigrapha,* ed. James H. Charlesworth, 2:250, 252.

20. Ryszard Rubinkeiwicz, "Abraham, Apocalypse of" in *Anchor Bible Dictionary,* 1:42.

21. C. Burchard, "Joseph and Aseneth" in *Old Testament Pseudepigrapha,* ed. James H. Charlesworth, 2:186.

22. S. L. Greenslade, "English Versions of the Bible, 1525-1611" in *Cambridge History of the Bible,* ed. S. L. Greenslade, 3:169.

Index

About The Author

Howard Cox was educated at Pennsylvania State University, Harvard University, Union Theological Seminary (NY), and Princeton Theological Seminary. He served as minister of the Fort Hamilton Presbyterian Church in Brooklyn, NY, Chaplain to Methodist students at Princeton University, Instructor in Old Testament at Princeton Theological Seminary, and Professor of Old Testament at Moravian Theological Seminary. During his teaching career, his publications concentrated on the personal Bible with commentary of Johann Sebastian Bach, material that he authenticated and published in the book *The Calov Bible of J.S. Bach* (UMI Research Press, 1985). By invitation, he presented his findings on the Bach Bible at the 300th Anniversary International Conference on Bach Research in Leipzig, Germany, in 1985. He has also published numerous articles on the subject.

The current book represents his independent reflections on the Old Testament after teaching it to seminary students for 32 years.